Creating An Awesome You

A Young Adult's Guide

Diana Hutchison
Illustrations By Lara Korotenko

16pt

Copyright Page from the Original Book

Copyright © by Diana Hutchison.

All rights reserved. No part of this book may be used or reproduced by any means, graphic, electronic, or mechanical, including photocopying recording, taping or by any information storage retrieval system without the written permission of the publisher except in the case of brief quotations embodied in critical articles and reviews.

This edition published 2018 by DoctorZed Publishing.

DoctorZed Publishing
10 Vista Ave, Skye, South Australia 5072
www.doctorzed.com
orders@doctorzed.com

Because of the dynamic nature of the Internet, any web addresses or links in this book may have changed since publication and may no longer be valid. The views expressed in this work are solely those of the author and do not necessarily reflect the views of the publisher and the publisher hereby disclaims any responsibility for them.

The author of this book does not dispense medical advice or prescribe the use of any technique as a form of treatment for physical, emotional, or medical problems without the advice of a physician, either directly or indirectly. The intent of the author is only to offer information of a general nature to help you in your quest for emotional and spiritual wellbeing. In the event you use any of the information in this book for yourself, which is your constitutional right, the author and the publisher assume no responsibility for your actions.

Any people depicted in stock imagery are models and such images are being used for illustrative purposes only.

Cover imagery © Shutterstock

Printed in the United States of America, Australia & UK.

DoctorZed Publishing rev. date: 08/08/2018.

TABLE OF CONTENTS

Preface	ii
Foreword	v
Chapter 1: How to Use This Book	2
Chapter 2: Physical Health	15
Chapter 3: Family/Home life	47
Chapter 4: Relationships	76
Chapter 5: Sex and Sexuality	115
Chapter 6: Interests and Hobbies	131
Chapter 7: Finances	149
Chapter 8: Work/Career	180
Chapter 9: Emotional Life	203
Chapter 10: Mental Health	225
Chapter 11: Addictions	263
Chapter 12: Self-Esteem	291
Chapter 13: Assertiveness	310
Chapter 14: Personal Growth	332
References	357
Other Titles	373
Back Cover Material	375

This book is for my parents Elizabeth and Robert.

Preface

This book is a natural progression from my first book, *Setting Yourself Free*. It may well be helpful to have a copy of my first book with you to refer to, or even to read that one first before embarking on *Creating an Awesome You*. While *Setting Yourself Free* dealt with changing yourself and your life, *Creating an Awesome You* explores many different areas of life and looks at each one at its best expression. Thus, it encourages you to be your best in each area. If you manifest the potential expressed within, you will be creating an awesome you.

It is becoming more and more difficult to sort through the myriad of information out there in the ether, or the World Wide Web, and find the golden nuggets that can help to build your life. It is my hope that those of you who read this book can indeed find that nugget and take action to become your best, to fulfil your potential, and to create a wonderful life for yourself. As you will see throughout these pages

I talk about the individual within a social setting. No-one is isolated, we are all part of a larger whole: society, and humanity. It just depends on your beliefs and feelings as to where you put yourself within that setting.

I thank the many people who contributed to this book. Whether in providing personal stories, feedback or both, you have made this book much more alive and encompassing. Thank you too to my editor, Hari Teah, who helped me to expand my mind and thoughts around what the book should talk about. A big thank you also to my mentor, Miriam Henke, who provided great feedback and has written the foreword. Miriam is a health psychologist with a special interest in mind-body medicine in Adelaide. She is also an executive coach and NLP Master Practitioner and Trainer. Miriam holds the title of Senior Clinical Lecturer at the University of Adelaide and contributes to innovation through research supervision and in her teaching.

Not to forget the illustrator, Lara Korotenko, whose creativity and talent

makes the pages within so much brighter.
Happy reading!

Foreword

Adolescence and young adulthood is a significant transition period in a person's life. A time of growing independence and learning about the responsibilities, joys and pitfalls of adulthood. In previous generations, milestones like moving out of the family home, moving in with a partner or getting married are now being delayed until later in life. So, what's more important now to young people? According to the Australian Bureau of Statistics, young people are more interested in tertiary education (over half of young adults have non-school qualifications), being employed, travelling and having rich social experiences.

This important time of life is complicated by the influence of cultural pressures, social media, the schooling system (that has a bias towards tertiary education and generally doesn't teach young people life skills), the lure of drugs and alcohol, and growing minds and bodies. A big part of this period of development is the importance placed on discovering one's own identity and sexuality, friendships, romantic relationships and a career path. Young people are naturally quite self-absorbed and more likely to rebel against authority figures and parents in an effort to become their own person. This often leads to conflict with family and institutions (e.g. school, police), and can be a stressful time for those caring for the young person.

Parents, caregivers and educators know all too well the realities of the world and what adulthood means. Their well-meaning efforts to rein in a young person's risky behaviours and *laissez-faire* attitudes inevitably butt heads with a young person's developing ideals, impulses and values. In other words, it's a challenging time for everyone involved.

This book is a comprehensive set of guidelines for young people transitioning from childhood into adulthood; a time of great confusion, change, and pressure. What young people go through in their teenage years and early twenties is seriously intense. There's a lot to deal with day-to-day, let alone considering the future and what to do to prepare for the best future possible.

Being a teenager and young adult is easy for noone. Your body is changing, school is demanding and often a major drag, there's pressure on you from many sources (e.g. parents, teachers, friends, social media) to do well academically, in sports, in friendships, and contribute positively to your home and family life. Your teenage years are meant to be preparing you to become a functional adult in the 'real world'. However, many adults I know, including myself, felt that school simply didn't teach enough real-life skills.

Like all adults walking (or stumbling!) through life, we learn and figure things out as we go. Sometimes we get things right and sometimes we make mistakes. Life can be very hard. It can bring great suffering, pain and torment. Knowing how to overcome obstacles, deal with your emotions and issues, bounce back after failure, heal a broken heart, and live on very little are all invaluable skills worth developing as early on as possible. Life can also give you the sweetest of thrills, pleasures and priceless moments. Those delicious, fun, comforting, and beautiful things can bring both richness and reward, as well as addiction challenges and escapism.

You'll find that people will give you lots and lots of advice at this time. Most you won't want, will disagree with or completely ignore. There's a funny thing about the human mind that it will hear and take on the messages it needs, and it might need to be exposed to a particular message several times (and even over several years) before it gets taken in or acted on. We become awakened to ideas before we take them on, and if they appear to come from within us and align with our values, we're much more likely to act upon them.

I really believe Diana has written an extremely useful book to guide young people through the transition into adulthood with the information, wisdom, tools and tips needed to navigate a challenging yet incredibly rich time of life. This book is accessible, straightforward, judgement-free, and grounded in psychological research evidence. It's modern, relevant and will be a resource you can come back to time and again.

Without a doubt, a copy of this book will be gifted to each of my children on their 16th birthday. I want my kids to have something I didn't have when I was young, but something I wish I did have; the information not taught at school which you really need to truly be your best self and have an awesome life.

Miriam Henke

1

Chapter 1

How to Use This Book

Welcome to the creating an awesome you! Each chapter explores a different area of life, and how to be the best in that area.

Before we begin, let me introduce myself. I have a background in psychology, and have now moved into counselling and life coaching. I specialise in grief and loss, health and wellbeing, and relationship counselling, and am an NLP Master Practitioner.

I have written this book because it would have been wonderful to have had access to something like it as I moved through my teens and into adulthood. I believe gaining these insights during those years would have started me on the road to self-awareness and self-development much earlier in life. I hope that it helps you to explore the way you think and feel about your life, and how you want it to unfold. Using these insights can really help you to make your life happen in the best way for you. It does take some effort, but if you are able to plan and organise things then it is likely to have positive outcomes. Take charge of your life and don't allow your life to just happen to you – ensure you happen to it.

The best way to use this book is to read it chapter by chapter. You don't need to read the chapters in sequential order. You can read them in any order. Read a chapter, think about it, and if you have a friend or family member who is also reading it, then you could talk about it with them. It will be particularly helpful to do this if you are having some problems with the subjects discussed in that particular chapter.

Where a family member or friend has recommended that you read this book, trust that they have your interests at heart and give it a go. Here is a short summary of how to approach each chapter, so that you get the most out of the book:

CHAPTER 2 – PHYSICAL HEALTH

After you have read through this chapter, go back and work out which areas you believe you can improve on in your life. It might be diet, it might be exercise, it might be both. You may not have thought about the long-term consequences of your behaviour, but find that you would like to do so. Maybe you'd like to stay healthy over the long term, and find that you are willing to think about putting different behaviours in place. It is your life and you can have a major impact on how it pans out in the future. You now have the opportunity to change the way in which your life progresses. Make a conscious decision to become awesome. Then you will be living the best life you could wish for, and later on you will be thankful that you made such a choice.

Read the chapter, check out the recommended websites and make a list of things you can do to effect change. To find help in goal setting and general aspects to self-change, please refer to my previous book, *Setting Yourself Free*. You can download it from my website www.dianahutchison.com.

CHAPTER 3 – FAMILY/HOME LIFE

After reading this chapter, think about your upbringing, your values and the beliefs you hold. Download the *values* and *core beliefs* forms and complete them. This will provide you with some information that you can act on, should you wish. Discuss your results with a family member or friend. Think about where you fit into your family, school and wider community. Also consider your 'in group' and 'out group'. Your 'in group' consists of a group of people whose characteristics mean that they get certain privileges. While society sets some of these, you can also set your own 'in group' and 'out group' based on your ideas of inclusion and exclusion. Are you encompassing values of compassion for yourself and others?

CHAPTER 4 – RELATIONSHIPS

After reading through this chapter, consider the relationships you have right now and see them in the light of your feelings about them. Are they strong? Are they loving? Do you know them well? Do you communicate well? Are you in a healthy relationship, or is it encroaching on your sense of self and not allowing you to breathe? Get a sense of where you stand and where your relationships fit into your world. Family, friends and partners.

CHAPTER 5 – SEX AND SEXUALITY

Reading this chapter will help you to form a clear idea of your sexual needs and desires, so that you can form healthy and positive sexual relationships with yourself and with others. Communication is important so that you know where you stand, and so that you can ensure you and your partner are comfortable and happy with your choices. Whatever your sexual identity, orientation or preferences you are not alone. Ensure you get support and ask for help when you need it.

CHAPTER 6 – INTERESTS AND HOBBIES

Make a note of the interests and hobbies that you really enjoy. This may give you an indication of the things that will stay with you through life or even point to something that might be a career. It would be helpful to explore your talents since these may well indicate the direction your career should go. Not everybody knows their passions when they are young, but if you do, then factor these in to your life plans.

CHAPTER 7 – FINANCES

Reading this chapter will give you a base from which to start good money habits. Ensure you budget and work out your financial position. Then you'll have the ability to assess whether you can save some money for things you might want, rather than only ever having enough for the things you need. The important thing is to shop around for the best deal you can get.

Rein in your credit card debt and take steps to ensure you are not spending more than you have coming in. The exception to this is if you are on Social Security payments. There are ways of saving money that you can engage in. Investigate the suggestions outlined for you.

CHAPTER 8 – WORK/CAREER

When you read this chapter, think about what you came up with in Chapter 6. Are you interested in pursuing a career doing something you loved as a child, in an area you found interesting, and that you have a talent for? Complete Holland's career interest survey and see what comes up. Check out the careers that match your top three highest areas and discuss them with your parents or friends. It's helpful to have a fall back position if your first love does not work out.

Work relationships are best if they are respectful. Where bullying occurs then there should be steps that you can take to seek redress.

It is positive if you can be assertive with your work colleagues.

CHAPTER 9 – EMOTIONAL LIFE

Throughout this chapter you will find information about the positives and negatives of emotions. Read about how to manage emotions, and how to process them. Learn how to be happy in the present moment. There is discussion of a variety of positive and negative emotions, whether they are useful, and if they are not, how to let them go.

CHAPTER 10 – MENTAL HEALTH

If you or someone you know has issues with anxiety, depression, psychosis, eating disorders or phobias, then you may already have some knowledge and information about some of the points discussed here. There is also information about possibilities for treatment. If you are not someone who has such issues then you may be thankful. The chapter may be useful for your reference should anyone you know have these issues.

CHAPTER 11 – ADDICTIONS

This chapter explores a number of addictions, such as tobacco, alcohol, prescription abuse, drugs, pornography, gambling, social media and gaming. There is also a general process of how to become free from your addiction, should you so desire.

CHAPTER 12 – SELF-ESTEEM

Everyone can read and discuss this chapter. If you have completed the core beliefs survey, downloadable from my website, then you will be able to note how high or low you have rated your self-esteem. See if you still rate it the same after reading through the characteristic behaviours of someone with low self-esteem. Pick and choose how you might improve your self-esteem through some positive self-talk. You can work out what you could say to yourself that will counteract your negative self-talk.

CHAPTER 13 – ASSERTIVENESS

Read about the differences between passive, assertive and aggressive behaviours. Work out where you are, and then you can work on becoming more assertive. If you are passive then often the first step is to begin to say 'no' in some situations. Becoming assertive means that you are standing up for yourself, meeting your needs and taking others' needs into account as well. It takes some effort and practice, but it is possible to become assertive. Even if you are often aggressive, you can learn to become assertive instead, so that you do not discount others' needs. Practice with the use of 'I statements', by asking for help, and by saying no.

CHAPTER 14 – PERSONAL GROWTH

Hopefully, personal growth is something you aspire to. Reading this chapter should get you into the frame of mind that enables you to think about what goals you'd like to set each year for your personal growth. People usually like to feel that they are moving forward. Setting goals can assist these feelings. The incorporation of positive psychology exercises will benefit your emotional growth and also help your relationships. Make sure that you pay attention to your intuition as you go about your daily life.

Once you have read through all the chapters in the book, and have begun working through your issues to become the person you want to be, you will be well on your way to creating an awesome you.

Personal change is an ongoing process, so the more you work on yourself, the more awesome you will become.

Be the best that you can be, and you will have an awesome life!

Chapter 2

Physical Health

QUALITY OF LIFE

Physical health is an important aspect of wellbeing and quality of life. Wherever you are on the spectrum of health, from those who have chronic conditions or disabilities, through to those who are at the peak of physical fitness, everyone should regard their health as a priority.

The choices we make and the things we do always have consequences, and some may have long-term effects. If you look after your body then you are giving yourself the greatest opportunities to be the best you can be. Everything you put into your body will have an effect on you and your life, so it is always best to make an informed decision about the things you do.

One part of the body affects the whole. Even the common cold makes most people feel miserable. The mind affects the body and the body affects the mind. A physical therapy such as acupuncture will affect how you feel both in your body and in your mind. A mental therapy such as cognitive behavioural therapy can help how you feel in terms of mood, and this can have an impact on your behaviour. As you feel better, you behave in different ways according to the context around you.

PHYSICAL FACTORS AFFECTING HEALTH

From the moment of conception, your physical environment and the nutrition you receive have an effect on your health. Early environments may pave the way for particular issues or problems later in life (1). However, although you can't change the circumstances of your birth, as you grow up you can choose your behaviour to give yourself the best chances in life, by looking after yourself, having a well-balanced diet, exercising, and getting enough sleep (1).

GUT HEALTH

Recently, the importance of gut health on both the body and mind has come into prominence. The microbiome (the gut environment with the different bacteria) affects health in many ways, and so may be at the root of a variety of illnesses and diseases. Thus, diet is very important and is the first thing to be explored in functional and integrative medicine. Functional and integrative medicine looks at the whole person, including diet, lifestyle, and symptoms, and utilises all possible avenues for healing.

So, what can you do to help ensure your physical health is the best it can be? Everybody is different, so you may need to take a little time to work out what is right for you and your body, and some of those things may change at different points in your life, but by and large there are some basic rules that you can follow. Firstly, if you have a course of antibiotics, ensure that you follow-up with a good probiotic to replace the good bacteria in your gut. Secondly, diet is particularly important.

We are what we eat. Thirdly, the reduction and elimination of toxins is also important.

Food For Thought

DIET

What you put into your body forms the foundation of what nutrients your body is able to extract, and what it can do with them. Actions include using the energy from the food immediately, storing the energy until later or getting rid of it. Because your body will not reject food that isn't off or bad in some way, it is important to do your body's thinking for it. Are your food choices at least relatively healthy? Are the things you eat not very good for you? Are you eating the right amount? Eating too much or too little can be damaging to your body. You can find out more about eating disorders in Chapter 10.

Whatever you eat, chew it well. There is some evidence that the more you chew your food, the more you will feel full and thus not eat as much (2). So chew a mouthful about thirty times rather than fifteen (which is usual). If you were ever told to chew your food instead of wolfing it down, you were given good advice.

Most authorities tend to say that it is better to eat food that is closest to its natural state. There may be those for whom cooked is better, but the fewer additives and processes the better. It is well-recognised now that processed meat in large quantities causes a higher risk of cancer. Therefore, you could limit the amount of ham, bacon, sausages, salami and other processed meats you eat to reduce this risk (3).

Vegetables should be as fresh as possible. Some people prefer organic vegetables and fruit. There are more shops allowing for this option now than ever before. Frozen vegetables are fine, too, although freezing may cause some loss of nutrients. It might be healthier to limit your meat intake to a few meals per week. By including some meals of fresh fish you will also be getting some Omega 3s. Generally, processed food and junk food should be eaten only rarely.

IDEAS AND BELIEFS

We eat for sustenance and energy, but meals can often have a social element, too. As a result of this, food and drink have become laden with ideas and beliefs around cultural and social situations. Eating meals together can be a bonding experience and this can make a positive contribution to our wellbeing.

Eating may also have a moral element. Some people choose to be vegetarians because they have a belief that killing animals for consumption is wrong. There may also be concerns over the method of killing, or the fear and suffering that the animals feel.

Where the belief is that any sentient being and products should not be eaten by humans, the most usual choice is veganism. As well as not eating meat or fish, vegans don't eat eggs or dairy, as they are animal products. This reflects a philosophy that rejects the commodity status of animals, and the exploitation of them (4).

It is an individual choice to be a vegetarian or vegan, as it is to follow any kind of diet. However, whatever diet you choose, it is important to ensure that you are getting all the nutrients you require. If you have dietary restrictions, supplements or some other way of fortifying your diet may be necessary to ensure a balanced diet. Investigation and planning is a good idea.

THE APPLICATION OF SCIENCE

The best diets are those backed by science. The Mediterranean Diet, and the CSIRO Wellbeing Diet are cases in point.

Studies that have been carried out on various diets appear to show that the best diet to feed yourself is the Mediterranean Diet. This is a diet rich in fruit and vegetables, legumes, whole grains, nuts, olive oil, fish, low in red meat, and low in sugar. The benefits of this diet have not only been shown to alleviate depression (5), but it also improves longevity and cardiovascular health, and reduce the risk of diabetes (6,7,8).

The CSIRO Wellbeing Diet was devised by the CSIRO scientists in Australia (9). It is based on healthy food, and reduced carbohydrates. Small portions are a feature.

FOOD FADS AND FASHIONS

Fad diets are just that!

Over time different diets may be in vogue and people may try them. Sometimes the diets may have a good aspect to them, but may not be helpful overall. A lot of fad diets may help you to lose weight over a certain period of time, but not be good over a long-term basis. So keep this in mind if trying out a fad diet. It's a good idea to scrutinise the levels of nutrition in the diet and to ensure that you are getting all you need.

THE FOOD PYRAMID

The food pyramid (10) refers to the recommended food groups and has not changed much over time. The highest proportion of our diet should be made up of fruit, vegetables and legumes, followed by grains, then dairy, then a small proportion of healthy fats. As far as drinking goes, water is the best choice. Reduce or cut out sugary drinks. Also cut out energy drinks which just contain a lot of sugar and a lot of caffeine. The food pyramid suggests that we should eat five serves of vegetables and two serves of fruit a day. This shows that fruit and vegetables should be a major part of your diet.

To form good eating habits, home-cooked meals are best. Ensure that you wash what you eat, whether you cook it or not. You can make tasty, cheap meals fairly quickly, and even though some meals may take longer to prepare, the reward is in knowing they are better for you than junk food, and that your friends or family can meet together around the table to eat. This helps communication and enhances your relationships.

A balanced diet should consist of foods from the food pyramid in the recommended proportions. If you have mostly home-cooked meals and rare meals of junk food then you are doing well.

SLEEP

It is also important for your health to get enough sleep. Sleep allows you to process the previous day's events, refreshing both the mind and body. You should be getting about seven to eight hours sleep a night. If you are getting less then you are probably operating at less than 100%. Tiredness can lead to bad judgements, memory issues, stress, and long-term health issues. Get into a routine of winding down before you go to bed (11). Melanin helps us get to sleep, and you can train your brain to get into the production of melanin earlier in the evening by turning off bright artificial lights for a few hours before you go to bed. It is recommended to stop using phones and computer screens for at least an hour before going to bed, and it also helps to go outside for a walk to get some early morning sunshine shortly after you get up (12).

Getting enough sleep is crucial to good health. On the other hand, it is possible to get health problems if you sleep for more than ten hours a night.

Those who sleep for this long are more likely to suffer with high blood sugar and diabetes. Oversleeping is also linked to negative thinking and depression. Since over-sleepers move less, there is the likelihood of obesity. Additionally, there is an increased risk of cardiovascular disease, for women as opposed to men (13).

TIPS

- Buy wholemeal or wholegrain bread instead of white bread
- Reduce fast food
- Home cook your meals
- Drink water
- Reduce or cut out sugary drinks
- Cut out energy drinks
- Follow the food pyramid
- Eat sensible portion sizes – smaller to lose weight
- Chew your mouthfuls for longer
- Get enough sleep

WEIGHT

Your body has an idea of the weight you should be. A recent experiment increased the food intake of people who were normally lean over a period of four weeks. They put on a bit of weight, but not as much as expected, and they lost it again in fairly quickly after the experiment ended. This also works the other way. If obese people lose weight, then unless they really change their eating habits and lifestyle in order to change the body's idea of the weight it should be, then the weight will just go back on (14).

> When Kylie was twenty-five she was nearly 100kgs and had very high blood pressure. She got read the riot act by her doctor. He said if she didn't change her lifestyle then she'd go to an early grave. This was a wake-up call. Her response was to change her diet, and to replace happy hour with walking. She lost 30kgs in eight months. She got fit. She recently ran in a half-marathon, and has never been healthier in her life.

The percentage of obese people in our society is increasing. The use of fats and sugars in shop-bought foods probably plays a part in this, as well as poor dietary habits. Childhood diet may have a role too, by giving the body the ideal weight concept.

While a weight-loss diet may help people to slim down in the short term, unless there are lifestyle changes and long-term changes in dietary habits, the weight just goes back on. There is now evidence that the reason for this is that hormones in the body cause the person to be hungry. In order to make long-lasting changes you can start making healthy decisions (15). Becoming fit is a good goal and a great achievement, but exercise by itself may not be enough to help you lose weight. You may need to change what you eat, when you eat, and how much you eat. Cutting right back on fast foods will help, or even cutting them out altogether, if possible. Home-cooked meals may require some extra planning and take a up a little more of your time, but improving your diet and nutrition should provide you with extra energy, meaning you can get more done with less effort, so things should soon balance out.

If you put yourself on a program to lose weight it is important to address your mindset, as well as your diet and exercise regime. If you monitor your physical weight then you could also monitor your psychological wellbeing. This can be done with the help of a psychologist or NLP Practitioner. NLP stands for Neuro Linguistic Programming, and it may be helpful in the process of weight loss, as it helps the conscious mind and the unconscious mind to align, so that automatic behaviour may be changed. This can make achieving your goals a lot easier than just using will-power.

ONE POPULAR WAY TO LOSE WEIGHT

Intermittent fasting, or the 5:2 diet, was made popular by Michael Moseley (16) What you do is eat normally for 5 days in the week, and choose 2 days in which you restrict your calorie intake to 600 calories. There is some evidence that this diet works and helps those who are overweight to lose weight, as well as reducing disease markers in the form of lowering cholesterol, blood pressure and blood sugar (17). If you also start choosing to eat a greater proportion of healthy food and less junk food then you may find extra benefits and improvements in your general health too. This diet helps weight to drop slowly, which is much better for your body than losing it rapidly, and makes it more likely to keep the weight off, provided you make some lifestyle changes.

DIETARY RESTRICTIONS

Having dietary restrictions may be difficult, especially when socialising and going out for meals. The situation may be easier when only one or two foods need to be avoided, but if there are a number of foods then it may become more complicated. When it comes down to quality of life, and is a matter of health and wellness, this is obviously important, and decisions can be made with such things in mind. You may need help, support and understanding from friends, family, and professionals, to ensure you are able to get the most out of your social life, in spite of the restrictions you face. Your doctor or health practitioner should be able to advise you of resources that can offer you help and support.

SUPPLEMENTS

Should you take supplements? Vitamins and dietary supplements are big business. There is some evidence that if you have a varied and healthy diet then supplements may well be a waste of time and money (18). Exceptions to this appear to include Omega 3 and vitamin D, and pregnant women should also take folate, iron, and iodine (which is in iodised salt). It may even be helpful to start taking these before pregnancy. However, with Omega 3, actually eating oily fish is probably better. So, actual foods are more beneficial than taking supplements. If you aren't eating the foods, or you are deficient in the nutrients, then supplements may be the best way to go.

It might be helpful to have Omega 3 if you have rheumatoid arthritis.

Studies have shown inconclusive results for any other benefits. It might also be helpful to have vitamin C if you smoke and vitamin B if you are stressed. Some people may be low in vitamin D, and this can be helped through supplements or a daily dose of sunlight. If you are interested in finding out more about supplements and feel that they may be of benefit to, you could discuss your situation with your doctor. You may also have a blood test and see what your doctor recommends.

Supplements may also be taken for muscle gain. Preparations containing protein, vitamins, and minerals may help this process. These need to be taken at the same time as working out. However, it depends on the results you want. You may choose to eat a healthy diet without taking supplements, which is the best option. While being strong can be a great goal, it is quite possible to be strong without having huge muscles, and it is always good to keep everything in balance.

ALTERNATIVE TREATMENTS

There are a number of alternative options to explore if you are not having any luck with conventional medicine. From a nutritionist, to a naturopath to an acupuncturist, you may be able to find the modality that works for you. An osteopath may be a good alternative to a chiropractor for skeletal issues and soft tissue problems.

DISABILITIES

No matter what type of disability you have, you are a normal person managing life the best you can. If you are a carer, then you have the exceptionally important job of caring for your loved one or client.

When you have a disability then there may be specific services and needs that you have that, if fulfilled, will enable you to gain optimal functioning and wellbeing. With the National Disability Insurance Scheme coming online in Australia it is to be hoped that you will find your needs are better met and that you will feel more included in your community. Everyone deserves respect and understanding, and social inclusion is an important concept for society to engage with on all levels.

While you may be restricted in some ways, you still have the potential to live your best life. Your beliefs about yourself can have a big impact on your world, as well as your physical restrictions. By giving yourself every opportunity to look after your physical health and wellbeing, you give yourself the best shot at reaching, and remaining, at the top of your game.

CHRONIC CONDITIONS

Whatever chronic condition you have, whether an autoimmune disease, chronic pain, or other disease or disorder, then you are no doubt attempting to manage it in the best way you can. It may take many trips to the doctor or specialist before you find something that helps your condition or allows you to be in the best space possible. Your health is likely to be a major concern and priority. If you have good days and bad days then you work towards having more good days. If there is anything you can do to make more good days, then you do it. Sometimes though, it may seem a bit unpredictable.

You may be on many medications and be at risk of addiction to painkillers. Where you have a good support network, you will be in a better position than someone who is isolated. So work on your friendships and family relationships in a positive manner.

It is important to ask questions of your medical support team. Be assertive, ask for information, and question them about how they came to suggest specific things. Question the side effects of medications and make sure that you are on the best ones for you. Medication only reduces symptoms; it is not a cure. Different medications have varying effects on individuals, even when they are in the same family of medication. So ensure you are on the medication that has the least side effects that controls your symptoms the best.

RECENT TRENDS

In recent times there has been a rise in autoimmune disease, food intolerances and allergies in the Western world. An inflammatory response occurs when the immune system's natural response to an external threat, whether bacteria or virus, is triggered, but there is no real threat. The body can, over time, have a chronic low-grade inflammation. You may or may not notice symptoms. Symptoms may arise in autoimmune diseases, food intolerances, or allergies.

In autoimmune diseases such as arthritis, multiple sclerosis, lupus, type 1 diabetes, Graves Disease (affects thyroid), and inflammatory bowel disease, the body is already primed, and has a chronic inflammatory response. Eating foods that cause inflammation may exacerbate the condition. Eating foods that are anti-inflammatory may be of benefit both in the short term and long term.

Food intolerances and allergic symptoms may range from mild to life threatening. It is possible to have a food intolerance, but not actually be allergic to the food. This is because there is a cut-off point between them. However, both food intolerances and allergies can lead to chronic low-grade inflammation. Allergies do not necessarily cause an anaphylactic response that is life threatening. When this is the case, a shot of adrenaline is necessary. Other responses and reactions may require changes to your diet. For example, when I was young, I was allergic to cow's milk and egg white, and the reaction to these foods was that I developed eczema. While the eczema disappeared over time, it took many years to disappear completely. Over time, I became less allergic to these foods.

If you have some symptoms and you suspect that you might have a food intolerance, then there is something that you can do about it. A doctor or a naturopath may be helpful in defining the actual problem. Alternatively, you can take yourself off the particular food for three weeks. At the end of the three weeks you reintroduce the food and make a note of the effects, and any symptoms you get. Compare how you felt during the three weeks you were off the food and how you feel being back on it. If there is no discernible difference, then perhaps the food is OK for you.

> **Foods more likely to cause an inflammatory response**
> Dairy, meat from grain-fed animals, processed/cured meats, alcohol, vegetable oils, artificial sweeteners, sugar, refined grains such as white flour and rice, trans fats, saturated fats (19).

> **Anti-Inflammatory Foods**
> Olive oil, green leafy vegetables, nuts, fatty fish, fruit including berries, tomatoes, garlic and onions, herbs and spices (20).

SELF-HEALING

Evidence is gathering that people can heal themselves through the power of belief and the power of the mind. The placebo effect has been known for a long time, and is taken into account in studies researching the effectiveness of medication. As Joe Dispenza suggests, 'You are the Placebo' (21). Self-healing is not necessarily a cure. It may, however, allow you to get to a much better place, and may alleviate some symptoms. It very much depends upon individual circumstances and individual responses. Some conditions are also more amenable to self-healing than others. Although it seems that some people manage what can be seen as a miracle, because it is the power of the mind that helps, the best way to effect self-healing is to work on your unconscious mind (22).

EXERCISE

Exercise is activity requiring physical effort, carried out to sustain or improve health and fitness.

Among the different activities that provide exercise, there are possibilities to exercise alone or in groups. You can also engage in exercise individually but among others, such as in a gym. Team sport is an exercise activity, as is cycling. There is an abundance of choice of exercise, and it comes down to your decisions about what works for you.

> The World Health Organization (23) recommends that adults aged between 18 and 64 engage in at least 150 minutes of moderate exercise each week. This exercise can be any activity: leisure time physical activity, such as dancing; transportation, such as walking or cycling; household chores, such as vacuuming; sports, such as soccer; or planned exercise, such as going to the gym. An alternative is to do at least 75 minutes of vigorous intensity aerobic physical activity throughout the week. For the best results, you should increase moderate intensity physical activity to 300 minutes per week or vigorous aerobic physical activity 150 minutes per week.

WHAT'S IN IT FOR ME?

There are numerous benefits to taking regular exercise. Many studies have shown that exercise improves cardiorespiratory and muscular fitness, and helps bone health. Additionally, those who are more active have lower rates of coronary heart disease, high blood pressure, stroke, type 2 diabetes, metabolic syndrome, colon and breast cancer, and depression. There is also less risk of hip fracture or vertebral fracture, and more likelihood of achieving weight maintenance and having a healthier body mass index (24). Regular exercise also improves chronic conditions and cognitive function. All in all, it makes good sense to exercise as much as possible.

HEALTH BENEFITS

The effect of exercise is, to some extent, an individual response. It appears that there may be a small percentage of people who do not respond to exercise by losing weight (25). This group still get the other health benefits of exercise, so there is no reason to despair if you seem to be in this small category. You can still exercise for fitness and look at making dietary changes to help support weight-loss.

Studies have also been done on life expectancy and sedentary lifestyle – results show that those with a sedentary lifestyle are at greater risk of dying earlier than those who exercise more. These are some good reasons to get into exercise!

RECENT RESEARCH

Recent research into exercise and its effects has shown that perhaps it is not necessary to exercise for as long as has been suggested in the past to gain benefits (26). There is now the idea that High Intensity Interval Training (HIIT) can be almost as good as exercising for longer periods of time. One particular routine that you can do consists of five minutes exercise three times a week. This involves the following:
- A little slow jogging on the spot to warm up, then
- One minute of star jumps, as quickly as possible

- One minute of squats, as quickly as possible
- One minute of sprinting on the spot, as quickly as possible
- One minute of star jumps again, as quickly as possible
- One minute of squats again, as quickly as possible

You can do this routine at home. It will cost you no money and it will improve your fitness.

Another aspect is that running is not as bad for your joints as you may think (26). After thirty minutes of running, you may feel a high from the increase of naturally occurring chemicals endocannabinoids in your brain. This chemical has a similar structure to that of cannabis, but because the increase is only about 30% there is a high without any damaging effects (26).

So think about engaging in either or both of these exercise routines to enhance your fitness and health. With both of these programs, make sure that you work up to the full exercise slowly, especially if you are unfit

MAKING CHANGES

As you go about your day, you can make changes that will help you to be fitter. You could use the stairs instead of the lift, and walk or cycle rather than driving, if the journey is not too far. It all adds up. Exercise doesn't necessarily have to be in large blocks of time. Even housework provides moderate exercise.

If you play a sport then you are probably getting the right amount of exercise in your week. Whether you participate in a sport or attend an exercise class you are making good, healthy choices that will be beneficial in the long term.

TIPS

- Take the stairs when you can
- Walk for 30 minutes a day
- Go cycling when you can
- Book into an exercise class – we are more motivated when others are involved
- Remember that every little bit adds up
- Play a sport of some kind

> • Make an exercise plan and stick with it

MAKING DECISIONS

It will be easier to make good decisions if you have your health as a top priority. It is a value that you can make important. When you need to make decisions about what you eat or drink, then you can ask yourself the question, 'Is this part of a balanced diet?' Such decisions need to be made at the time you can influence the outcome, so when you are making a shopping list, when you're shopping or when you're in a café, bar or restaurant. The same applies to exercise – do you really need to take the bus or the car, or could you walk or cycle instead? It's important to look at the long-term benefits rather than merely the short term emotions or convenience. Keep your health high on your agenda and make informed decisions.

Even small changes such as walking to the local shops instead of taking the car or eating whole grains, such as wholemeal bread or brown rice rather than white bread or white rice, will be beneficial. Making healthy decisions means that you are acting in the present for your future.

BECOMING AWESOME

- Eat a balanced diet
- Take regular exercise
- Limit your alcohol intake
- Abstain from cigarettes and drugs
- Eat nutrient rich food rather than taking supplements, wherever possible
- Get enough sleep
- By taking these steps, you give your body the best opportunity to achieve and maintain your most awesome physical health!

Chapter 3

Family/Home life

A family unit, into which a child is born, may nowadays consist of a variety of possibilities. The unit itself may change over time, and such a change may have consequences for the child's development. A family may consist of all the individuals under one roof or in the household. Sometimes it includes people who live apart from a household and who are most involved in a child's formative years, and who can be seen as primary caretakers. A family may be a traditional unit with a mother and father, or may be a single parent, blended family, or same sex couple unit.

THE IMPORTANCE OF FAMILY

The first seven to twelve years of life are very important in setting the tone for the rest of our lives. These are our years of growing up in all senses:

physically, mentally and emotionally. The groundwork is laid down.

There is evidence to indicate that temperament is innate or in your genes. So this means that if you are warm then you will get more positive responses in a social sense than if you are cold and show very little response to others. I would suggest that personality traits are the innate tendencies mixed with childhood experiences, where the innate tendencies may be a lot more detailed than just temperament. There may be talents and interests that just need to be nurtured in the early days.

There appear to be a certain number of characteristics that are set at birth, but there are also a fair proportion that are due to the environment. The current thinking on the nature/nurture debate appears to be that there is an integration of the two aspects in the expression of any particular characteristic, disease, or phenotype (1). Very few genes control anything alone, and there are usually a number of genes implicated. Genes may be either turned on or turned off. Thus, environmental factors play a large role in effecting the outcome of your experiences. This is why the early years are so important, and why having a loving and encouraging environment in a social sense is so important. If an individual has a good-enough early life this sets a good base to grow from. A good-enough upbringing means having overall positive experiences rather than negative experiences (2). Negative experiences may override the positive ones particularly if they are traumatic or complex.

Given that a baby is born with a nascent personality, then his or her personality is, to some extent, shaped by the experiences and incidences in his or her life as growth develops. You may be born as an extrovert and also be adventurous. This will mean that you are into everything as a young child, and that you will approach others rather than hold back. Thus, such experiences will shape your resulting personality. Whether you get rebuffed or not, or whether you get approval for such behaviour, will shape your future behaviour. Where you have more positive experiences here than negative, the good-enough experiences comes into play here and you will continue to approach others. Then you are likely to make friends more easily and so your personality grows.

NATURE/NURTURE

The issue of nature/nurture is still debated and researched. Despite some things being set, there is still a lot of room to move. While about 40% is inherited, a great deal of how you behave in situations is up for grabs. You can change your behaviour in many instances. You may have been born with talents that you can practise to become good at. If you are not assertive when young, then you can change and become more assertive. A pessimist may become more optimistic (3). While some difficulties and disorders may not be totally fixed, there is certainly room for improvement from the baseline. For example anxiety may be inherited, but management may mean at least moderate relief (4).

The environment of a child growing up is not only geological, but consists of the space of the immediate family, extended family, school, teachers, peers, media, church and religion, which all impinges on the curious and engaging mind of a child.

BELIEFS

As a child starts to make sense of his or her world questions are asked. Questions may be about things and animals, then later about why things are the way they are, how things work, and why. In this way, some sense is made of it all. In forming a world view, which grows over time, various beliefs are formed based on the explanations given from questions, and from interactions with the environment. We form beliefs about what happens and how the world is and about how other people are, and about who we are, based on our experiences. So a belief is a statement about what we think happens in our world (both external and internal). Interactions with others and what we are told about ourselves are crucial in forming beliefs. The more influence the person telling us about ourselves has on us, the more likely we are to believe it. However, the number of times we are told also affects how likely we are to take it on board.

Beliefs about ourselves are core beliefs (5). There are considered to be ten core beliefs. They are: self-esteem, safety, competency, control, lovability, autonomy, justice, belonging, trust, and standards. If you rate highly for all of these, or at least around the middle, then this is positive. It will depend on your circumstances as to whether you rate low, medium or high for these core beliefs. Sometimes, depending on recent past events, some may become lowered for a time. However, it will be best if you can overcome such changes so that you can feel better about everything. If you are interested in getting a rating of where you are in relation to these core beliefs, you can access a short survey at (6).

Since only you will know these results you can be honest. See what you get.

VALUES

Your parents and family are responsible for bringing you up, and this is where you get your ideas about yourself and the world, along with the later influences of preschool, day care, school and the children and adults you encounter along the way. This is how your values and beliefs about you, your life and the world are shaped. Your family is primary in you soaking up the values that are important to you in life. Values are the guiding principles of our life. It is helpful to sort out which values really are primary in your life. You can download a values survey at (7). Rate each value out of ten where ten is the most important. After you have rated each value, pick your top five. Values differ across individuals and within individuals over time. It is good to think about how you have these values in your life. How do you express that importance – how do you behave, what do you do? It varies across individuals in terms of the expression of any one value. For instance, for the value achievement, one person may be motivated to do really well on tests and exams and achieve success in their career, while another may seek achievement in terms of their collection of memorabilia.

If you have worked out your top five values and figured out how you incorporate those values into your life – as in what you do in relation to them – then you can start to think about how you view other people in relation to you, and just in general. Again, it is better to think well of others, at least those you come into contact with and those close to you. At the same time, it is important to be realistic since we cannot get away from the fact that there are some pretty destructive people in the world.

INTERCONNECTEDNESS

Beliefs and relationship with oneself impacts on how values are incorporated into our lives. If you believe that you are competent then you may value respect from others. If you believe that others lie and cheat then you are not likely to show respect to them.

So values, beliefs and, to some extent, attitudes to things are learnt in the home environment. As the child becomes older a revision of beliefs and attitudes may occur. This is likely to happen after different beliefs and attitudes are encountered during the child's school years, and particularly when the child becomes a teenager. This is a time when questions are asked and the teen places importance on peer relationships. If you negotiate this time in your life satisfactorily and manage to sort through all the contradictions and dichotomies presented to you, then you will maintain a good sense of yourself as a person.

HOME LIFE

Many young adults nowadays still live at home into their twenties and thirties. It is usually cheaper and more convenient to do this, rather than living away from home. However, it is to be hoped that if you are doing this that you are making a reasonable contribution to expenses and chores in an adult fashion, rather than still living as a dependant. When you are no longer a child you need to accept more adult responsibilities.

You could be contributing money towards rent, plus food money and something towards the cost of gas, electricity and water. You might want to work out a percentage that fairly represents your share. If you are not able to pay as much as this, then maybe you have come to a mutual arrangement with your parent(s) to ensure you are contributing as much as you can and, ideally, also able to save money.

If you are in a share house or are living with a partner then you are likely to have more expenses. It all depends on your situation – whether you are working, living away from home, how many people you are living with, and their relationship to you.

In whatever situation you find yourself in it is important to divide up the expenses as evenly as possible. If you are living at home perhaps you can do your own laundry, including your bed linen, and vacuum your room on a regular basis, as well as the rest of the house from time to time. Or you might clean the bathroom, sweep the yard, put out the garbage or any other chore. Chores are part of life, and even though we might resent having to do them, they help us get on with other activities and stop us living in squalor. While it might not be necessary to have an absolutely spotless house, it is preferable to have a generally clean house. This is for health and hygiene reasons. It doesn't take much time to vacuum, do the dishes, mop down the floors and so on. You can do one thing at a time, and once it is done you don't need to do it again for a while. So action rather than procrastination is called for.

If you are living at home you can negotiate with your parents regarding the chores you do that contribute to the household. You might cook a meal on a specific night or you might agree to do a couple of chores each week.

If you are in a share house then you might find it helpful to instigate house meetings and a roster for chores. It depends on whether you share food or not, regarding which chores will be on the list. It might be good to have a kitty for food in which you put so much money per week, and you could all go shopping together after you have made a shopping list. Then you could have a roster for who does the cooking and who does the washing up. It would be helpful if the roster also included house cleaning chores.

If you are living with your partner then you can have a meeting together and decide who is going to do what – and that doesn't have to be a hard and fast rule. Divide up the chores so that it is 50/50, rather than less or more.

MOVING OUT OF HOME FOR THE FIRST TIME

When you are ready to move out of home you need to think about a number of things. For example, can you afford it? To get a rental property it helps to have a permanent job with a reasonable income. Budget for your move and save up. On top of the rent, you need the bond money, which is usually four weeks' rent. Another question to answer is whether you are moving in with one or more friends, or by yourself. This relates to how many bedrooms are needed in your rental property and how expensive it might be. If you are moving in with friends, make sure to set up agreements around how you are going to share the expenses, whose name the utilities will be in, who will be taking up the lease, and whether the lease will be in one person's name or more. Estimate utilities and budget for water, gas and electricity per person, so you can all set aside enough money each week. You will need to supply yourselves with cutlery, crockery, pots and pans, bed linen, towels and other Manchester, as well as furniture. Work out who will contribute what in terms of kitchen things and furniture. Consider buying from op shops and second-hand shops, as you will save a lot of money. It's probably best to buy new bed linen and manchester for hygiene reasons, and you can pick them up at reasonable prices.

When looking for a rental property you need to put some time in. It takes a bit of organisation to get to the open inspections, have all the paperwork you need to put in an application for the property, and apply as soon as possible, if you are interested. Watch out for gazumping – being outbid by other applicants. If you have some good references and have good employment then you may have an advantage over others. However, it may take longer than you think to land yourselves a reasonable rental property.

When you have secured a rental property then you need to organise yourself and your friends into it. You will have a date from which the tenancy agreement begins, and you can move in after that, once you have the keys. While you may be able to move quite a lot of stuff just using your car, some bigger items may need to be moved by a removalist company or with a ute or trailer, which you may be able to borrow or hire. Moving in is another expense that needs to be thought of in advance and allowed for.

BELONGING & IDENTITY

Every human being wants to belong – to a family, a group, and a society. Human beings are social. We need each other to thrive.

It doesn't matter what racial background you have, you are part of many different groups, from the human race through to your family. In multicultural societies and countries like Australia, the UK or the USA it is becoming more important to accept everyone as part of your society. No-one is really different. Everyone has hopes and dreams, and each person should be respected as the unique individual they are.

All religious and political extremism that exposes hatred and violence towards others should be avoided. These views are not humanistic or helpful in adapting to human society as a whole. Extremist views aside, in the global village we now have, we need to accept each other's differences. You don't have to agree with everything other people say or feel, but it is important to remember that there is more that unites us than divides us. We are all the same underneath the skin, regardless of race, religion or colour.

Psychologically, we need to belong to a group. However, if we belong to a group then it follows that not everyone will necessarily belong to this group (apart from the group of humans). Thus, there is an 'in group' and an 'out group'.

The in group will have characteristics that are seen to be 'better' than those characterised by those considered to be the out group and will have privileges because of these. The in group then see themselves as better and may bully those not 'in'. An experiment in this context was first performed by Jane Elliot in 1968 in the USA (8). Rules were given to an out group and in group, and privileges were given to the in group. The teacher said that the kids with blue eyes were the in group. What happened was that the kids with blue eyes bullied those with brown eyes. The following day the teacher changed the rules and said that she had been mistaken, and those with brown eyes were actually better than those with blue eyes. So then the rules were reversed and all the kids in her class actually had the experience of both in group and out group. It was a salutary lesson.

It is just luck whether you belong to an in group or out group. No participant has any say in the matter. We should not blame those in the out group for being in the out group. Nor should we bully them for being themselves. We should see everyone as belonging to the group of the human race. Then no-one is in or out.

Characteristics that distinguish whether you are in or out are in fact quite arbitrary, just like having blue eyes or brown eyes. They are all aspects that come with birth, which we have no control over. Every human being has equal rights to you.

FITTING IN/BELONGING

At school, fitting in is usually a case of finding friends to hang out with and working out where you are with your values and beliefs about yourself. After you leave school, whether you go to work, university or college, this time is about working out where you fit in society. This may not necessarily be something you consciously seek, but it might nevertheless be a goal. If you can find something meaningful in your life then it might be your purpose. Where you can find what you love then doing this will help your life feel meaningful, whatever your interest is.

This is a time of working out what you believe in and working out how society works too. By degrees, it is possible to work out where you fit in to the larger world of social interaction. While there are varied ranges of beliefs and attitudes across society, not all are positive. You will be on the right track if you search for beliefs that enhance the human spirit and that do not engage violence, hate and revenge. If you look for beliefs that enhance the human spirit then you will find a more positive outlook, and increase your chances of helping others.

As you go about your daily life you will find that society has norms and rules about how to interact with others. Because we are social beings, there are ways of behaving that tend to make it easier to relate to and deal with people. One of these rules is manners. It is polite to say please and thank you, and will more than likely get you what you want faster, or at least get a smile. When meeting new people, be interested in them. You may wish to ask them questions about themselves. By asking questions, you may find out something that will help you or a way in which you can help them. Small talk helps to grease the wheels of social interaction. It can lead to deeper and more meaningful exchanges and can help you figure out if you have anything in common that might lead to a friendship. It is important to talk inclusively and in a way that doesn't exclude various groups of people.

Society expects you to behave responsibly when you are an adult. This means behaving sensibly and within the law. If you can figure out where and how you fit in – even if only a theory – then feeling comfortable in society will be much easier.

When Things Go Wrong

BREAKING THE LAW

If you break the law and it is a fairly minor crime, then you may only receive a caution or a fine. Getting into trouble with the police can feel very scary, and even a slight brush with the law may be enough to deter you from doing anything that will land you in trouble again. If you find yourself in this situation then it can be a good opportunity to make changes to your life that ensure you stay out of trouble in future.

If you break the law while you are under eighteen years of age and it is serious, or if you have been in trouble many times before, then you might end up in juvenile detention. Firstly, you'll be charged. Secondly, you'll be locked up in a police cell until the next business day when you'll go to court to be granted bail. Whether bail is granted or not, you will be arraigned for a future date. Arraignment is a formal reading of the charges against being brought against you. It is at this stage that you may get a legal aid lawyer to represent you in court. However, legal aid lawyers are run off their feet with cases and they may not be able to represent you in the way a private lawyer may be able to. In any case, you may need the evidence in your favour in order to have the best outcome. If you are granted bail then you are free to go back home, but you are obliged to attend court on the date that is set for your next hearing. You are not allowed to interfere with or have contact with any witnesses in the intervening time.

Where bail is not granted then you will be taken to a remand centre for juveniles. In such an institution everyone is all mixed up together waiting to come to trial for their charges. You will probably need to share a cell with someone else. You may or may not like them or get on with them. You may or may not get on with anyone there. There are likely to be power plays and even fights over seemingly inconsequential things. Even small things in the outside world get to be important in custody.

In juvenile detention you are restricted in where you can go and what you can do, and you are constantly reminded that you have lost your freedom. Visits only happen at certain times, such as weekends. You are only able to buy certain goods on buy-ups to take care of yourself and your habits. You will have no access to a mobile phone. If there are any computers, they will only be for use with educational courses, and not for personal use.

You will probably find that the officers are called 'the boss', or 'the chief', and that they have the say over everything while you are there. Roll call occurs at least twice a day. A cast iron bladder is a positive.

While there are some programs that are available in detention they are few and far between, so unless you want to do an educational course you will probably have little to do and be bored out of your brain. In any case, while on remand the time frame of staying there is uncertain and you will probably feel in limbo.

You will not like juvenile detention and it is not something to aspire to.

No-one will feel admiration for you going there and it is not something to big note yourself about.

ADULT GAOL

If you are eighteen years old or over when you commit a crime, then you will be sent into the adult prison system. What holds for juvenile detention is doubly true for the adult system. Both systems are hotbeds of crime. You can learn more about how to commit various crimes, and come out more of a hardened criminal rather than a reformed inmate. However, it is your choice and if you choose, you can make a gaol sentence your call to a better life. It is better if you make this call as a juvenile, but it will still work if you are in the adult system. Take your sentence as a wakeup call and don't give in to the easy way. You have the opportunity to take your life into your own hands and make something of it. It is not too late.

EXTREMISM

Extremism of any kind is often expressed by those on the margins of society. Stay within the central block that will still afford you a wide range of beliefs to choose from. Extremist beliefs are not enhancing to the human spirit and they do not help enable people to live together in the world.

How to recognise extremism:
- They have an exclusive 'in group' that they invite you to join
- They make you feel special for joining
- They may have an initiation or ritual to join
- You get to belong to a select group with special privileges
- They preach hate, violence, vilification and discrimination to those people in the 'out group'
- They invite you to break laws
- They may require action on your part for accessibility for special treatment

Joining for social reasons and to belong somewhere doesn't work in the long run – there are alternative groups that will provide better, more positive emotions.

The internet shows ranges of beliefs and attitudes, both politically and morally. Sites espouse views from the far left of politics to the far right, including Neo-Nazis views. Since anyone can set up a website there are sites espousing what can be called crackpot views and conspiracy theories. Be discerning and be careful. Sort out these sites, including the political extremes, so that you don't pay attention to them. A lot of sites cannot be trusted. It is better to pay attention to the sites that are more centrist and mainstream, especially if you are looking for balanced and accurate information.

Sites that talk about violence towards anyone and hold extreme views are not safe to explore, and it is dangerous to start to think like the people who create them and use them. Don't be swayed by what you read on these sites. You would be best served by staying away from such views and maintaining a humanitarian stance.

POLITICS

It is also a time to work out where you stand in the political sense. In Australia, where voting is compulsory, it is important to be aware of what you want to vote for. The issues that are important to you will be actioned if you vote for the party or people that have policies that address those issues. Become engaged and politically savvy. Your vote, along with others of your generation, will make a difference. Read up and watch the political news, work out who you agree with, and vote for them when you have enrolled to vote.

Firstly, enrol to vote when you turn eighteen years old. If you haven't enrolled yet and you are older, then do it now. Work out where you stand on party policy for each party, and vote accordingly. Some issues may be more important to you and so you might concentrate on your most important issues. It shouldn't just be about your own benefits, but rather the benefits of the many and of your country. Social justice should figure in your thoughts.

In other words, think of others and the larger picture, rather than just yourself.

Some people work hard to do the right thing by others. It is important to treat others the way you would like to be treated. It is not enough to treat others how they treat you. This is more likely to get you into a downward spiral of assuming something, acting on it, and not getting the results you were after in the first place. If you always treat others how you would like to be treated then this means that others will have a positive view of you and will therefore be happy with you, and you will be more likely to get the results that you want. It is, however, not just getting the best for yourself – if you always treat others how you would like to be treated then you are acting from a good humanitarian value base.

BECOMING AWESOME

- Move towards humanity and the humane, rather than the extremes.
- Become aware of the whole world rather than just your little world.

- Become interested in politics and the environment, and act on a local level. You may even inspire others.
- Think about social justice and follow your heart.
- Keep family relationships as positive as you can.
- By taking these steps you can start creating an awesome family or home life.

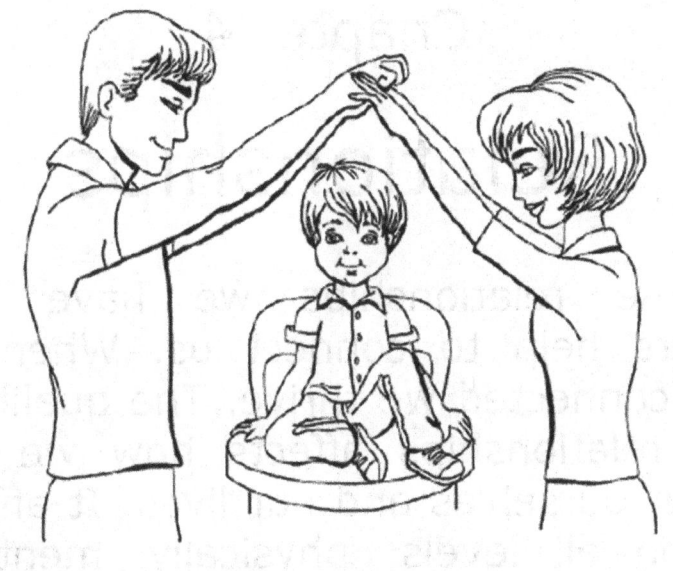

Chapter 4

Relationships

The relationships we have with others help to connect us. When we feel connected we thrive. The quality of our relationships affects how we feel about ourselves and our lives. It affects us on all levels: physically, mentally, emotionally, and spiritually.

The social support you have helps you through troubled times and allows you to be happier and healthier than otherwise. Recent evidence suggests that having four to five close friends makes for a happier and less lonely person (1,2). Additionally, those with partners or who are married generally have a better quality of life than those who are single (3).

It makes sense to work on your relationships because they are so important. Become the best friend you can be, become the best partner you can be, and as you change and grow within yourself so will your relationships change and evolve. The best relationship may occur where each person is accepted and respected for themselves and the relationship together continually evolves at the intersection point between.

FAMILY

It is important for a baby to feel cared for so that his or her needs are met, and if the needs are met most of the time then this is good enough parenting and the baby will have an overall positive experience. Security is essential for a baby and for a child. When a child is a bit older, it is important to set boundaries, so that then the child will be secure in knowing the limits of behaviour. This will mean that later on he or she will be able to be a well-functioning person in society and be able to set their own limits.

While Bowlby (4) first brought the idea of 'good enough' mothering into use and discussed attachment theory, Dan Hughes (5) is a more recent attachment theorist. A baby attaches to his or her attachment figures for comfort and safety; including for food, warmth and protection. The baby interacts with the attachment figures with eye contact, non-verbal communication and touch. The response a baby receives from his or her caregivers determines whether he or she becomes securely or insecurely attached. The response gained may be consistently welcoming and warm, or distant and irregular. Again, if the overall response is positive, then the baby will become securely attached. If generally the response is negative, then the baby will develop an insecure attachment. An insecure attachment may indicate a challenge to forging healthy relationships in life. A secure attachment in childhood means that the person can become an independent and autonomous adult. In this case, healthy relationships eventuate.

Through our attachment histories we tend to utilise generally consistent approaches to our relationships over time. Thus, patterns of thought, emotion and behaviour may be noticed over relationships, and between them too. Whatever your attachment pattern, it is possible to become more autonomous and independent as an adult and display more attributes of a secure attachment style (5).

A child with a healthy, secure attachment feels safe with their caregiver and in novel situations. Feeling safe sets a base from which to explore your world. In a secure attachment, the child is able to learn more about themselves and the world, since they feel safe to explore. In an insecure attachment, the child learns much less about themselves and the world, and learns less from his or her parents at the same time (5).

As an adult our attachments styles may be:
1. preoccupied, where a person is continually preoccupied with the relationship to the detriment of the relationship itself;
2. dismissive, where a person is dismissive of the relationship and minimises the extent of it and issues around it;
3. unresolved, where there is no coherent pattern and relationships are problematic

4. autonomous, where a secure attachment was formed as a baby. The person is independent and confident in relationships.

See (5) for an in-depth exploration of attachment, attachment styles and what you can do to become more secure and autonomous.

Family relationships are very important. If you received good enough parenting as a baby and child then you are likely to be secure in yourself, since your family relationships were stable and secure. Where family life was unstable for any reason as a young child, then you are more likely to feel less secure. And you may not feel as good about yourself as you otherwise would. Strong loving relationships with parents and siblings are ideal. Again, good enough family relationships are best, where positive feelings are generated rather than negative ones. Quarrelling with siblings is normal, just as long as it's not all the time.

Where you had more negative than positive experiences, had a dysfunctional family, or experienced traumatic events, all is not lost. Children are resilient, and from the vantage point of an adult many of these issues may be worked upon and the effects ameliorated to a reasonable extent. And any effects may or may not occur in the first instance (6). Asking for help from a trained professional would be important where there are effects.

You are not defined by those experiences that have not been helpful. There are relationships beyond the family that may be of more positive use. You can choose to use these as your positive point of reference. Negative feelings from relationship experiences are normal and are part of recognising what an unhealthy relationship is. So this is how you can use your negative experiences in a positive way.

BOUNDARIES

Boundaries are the limits set on acceptable behaviour. Boundaries should be put in place early so that a child is able to feel secure and safe. Parents can still be loving and set boundaries. When boundaries are set a child will be able to take responsibility for his or her actions, attitudes and emotions, based on his or her experience.

There are good boundaries and unhealthy boundaries. How do you recognise them? (7). Each person needs to have personal boundaries. These are limits on themselves and others, in relation to behaviour. To have healthy boundaries in place probably means that you are able to be assertive and relate your limits to others in a way that takes their needs into account, as well as yours.

In a family the parents keep a boundary around them (8). They share confidences and intimacy that they should not share with their children. They share more information with their children, but it is quite different. If personal information and confidences are shared with a child, then enmeshment occurs and the boundary that should exist between them is breached. Children do not know how to deal with adult confidences and should not be expected or asked to do so. Another form of enmeshment occurs when children are placed in a situation of acting as go-between or being asked to choose between parents.

Another unhealthy boundary situation occurs when there are few limits on behaviour (8). The child in this situation is unlikely to develop healthy personal boundaries and take responsibility for his or her actions. In fact, if the parents are permissive then the child may rebel because reliably enforced guidelines help them feel safe and secure.

No matter what your boundaries, see 'Ten ways to build and preserve better boundaries' (9). There are some good tips you can put into action now.

HOW TO SET BOUNDARIES

You can set boundaries for yourself or for others. I am talking here about healthy boundaries that help you feel safer, more together, whole and clear, not unhealthy restrictions or demands that you use to control other people. Setting healthy boundaries will not only help you, but will also allow the other person to feel you are respecting them as a person who can take responsibility for themselves. Each boundary needs to be stated in terms of behaviour and the limit being placed upon the person.

There also needs to be consequences for breaking the boundary. It is helpful to have perhaps three different consequences going from the first time to the third time, with increasingly hard consequences. For instance, a boundary might be that people should speak to you politely. The first infraction might get a warning of what will occur if there is a second time. The second time, perhaps the consequence is that the person loses a minor privilege. The third time, the person might lose something more important. The boundary needs to be set verbally with the person concerned and the consequences spelt out before you start counting infringements. For information on how to set boundaries for kids see (10).

You can also set a boundary for yourself. You may enjoy going to the pub with your friends. You may also need to get up early for work during the week. You might set a boundary so that you stay at home and go to bed early during the week, and only go to the pub on Friday and Saturday nights.

This boundary means you sometimes miss out on something that you enjoy, in order to ensure you can get up for work on time and have a clear head. You need to ensure that you stick to your rule and carry out the consequences when appropriate.

It's probably easier to set boundaries for others and stick to them than it is to stick to boundaries that you set for yourself. Even if you forget or ignore a boundary you have set for yourself, then it is still possible to put it in place next time. It does take a bit of effort but it may well be worthwhile.

ROLE MODELS

The family is a blueprint of how we relate to others in the world. Our parents model the behaviour, and we view this behaviour as the way to do things in a relationship. Your parents are your first role models. This relates to both the behaviour seen between parents as well as how parents behave towards you and your siblings. So as you grow up and have your own family, you might catch yourself behaving like your mum or your dad or whoever was your parental figure. While you may take your parents' behaviour as a model for your behaviour, it is also possible that you take their behaviour as a model of how not to behave. It could go either way. The process of using their behaviour as a model works quite well where you have had good enough parenting yourself, but can fall over where you haven't. In this circumstance, it is helpful to have a positive role model within your wider circle of extended family, friends, or community members.

Although our parents are our first role models, we may choose other role models when we are a little older. These are people we admire and want to be like. Such role models may be known to you through school, family connections or friends. It is helpful if you choose your role models carefully.

As we grow up, where we are straight and grow up in a straight two-parent family, we probably use the same sex parent as a role model, and use the opposite sex parent as an aspiration for an intimate relationship.

If you are female then you may find yourself attracted to men who are like your father in some way. If you think about it, there may be an issue that is repeated in your relationships with men your own age that was an issue between you and your father. Similarly, with men and their mothers. If you are homosexual then the issue may be similar to the same sex parent, but it might not. The issue may not necessarily be a problem, but it might indicate such things as characteristics you are attracted to, but there may be an underlying problem depending on the parents' behaviour. Psychologically, we are attracted to those people who will present us with the issues we need to resolve. So, if your father left the family home or died when you were young, then you may find yourself attracted to men who tend to abandon you. If this is the case then you could face the issue straight on and have counselling to resolve this. Once you resolve these issues you will be able to change the quality of partner you end up with. Similarly, if a man's relationship with his mother has been very intense then he may continue to have difficulties with partners. If there are issues, they will always be specific to the individuals involved. It is a good idea to look underneath the surface interactions in your relationships so that you can be aware of the undercurrents and the motives you have, as well as those that your partner has.

Your parents are likely to have your best interests in mind. Understand this when they warn you off from being with certain people and from doing certain things. Be willing to discuss all aspects and reasons why they think this way. The more they are willing to talk about it and explain their reasons, the more likely you may be able to understand, then you will be empowered to make the decision that is right for you. Give them the credit of having lived longer than you, and that their life experience affords them the knowledge that may guide you on the right path.

As we grow up we interact with our family members. Your ways of talking, in terms of what you say, how you say it, and when and why you say it, will depend on your family interaction experience. Were you continually put down for saying things or were you encouraged to speak your mind? Whatever pattern occurred in your family will have an effect on how you now communicate. Did your parents model good communication styles such as assertiveness? Was each family member given the space and respect to say their piece? There will be some effect of such practices on your ability and willingness to communicate with others. Even if there is only a small effect there will be an effect.

Teenagers can be particularly testing on family relationships. This is a time when they push the boundaries and are looking for their own identity apart from the family. The way parents respond to teenagers can have a big impact on the dynamics.

ALICE AND STEPHANIE

Alice was like Jekyll and Hyde when it came to the way she interacted with her daughter, Stephanie. Her husband once said that if he ever saw her behave with anyone else in the way she behaved with Stephanie that he would leave her.

Three years ago, Alice made a decision to start observing her mind. She was standing in the kitchen when Stephanie came home. Like most days, Stephanie spoke rudely.

In that moment, Alice made a decision to bite her tongue.

Normally, she would have reacted with instant rage. While standing in her own fury, she noticed that Stephanie had moved on in conversation. Before, they would have been yelling. Again, Stephanie spoke rudely, and again, Alice bit her tongue. Stephanie didn't notice that Alice wasn't reacting.

The next morning, they enjoyed a coffee together. Usually, they wouldn't have spoken for a week.

As Stephanie's rudeness continued, Alice continued to bite her tongue. She'd move on in conversation and she became less reactive. It was like an ignited fuel tank was emptying inside of her. Each time she bit her tongue she became less reactive.

After this had been going on for a week, Stephanie spoke rudely to Alice and Alice looked up with a smile and said, 'I love you.' Stephanie replied, 'Now I know you have officially lost it.'. In that moment, Alice realised she was no longer being reactive.

The more Alice bites her tongue, the more intuition she receives to help situations, and the greatest reward is that her relationship with her daughter gets better every day.

SCHOOLING PLUS

There will also be an effect on your relationships based on your experiences at school. And your personality will have impacted on your school relationships. Things such as whether you find friends easily or not, whether you become popular or not, and whether you are bullied or not. Possibly, your respect for your parents will relate to the respect you have for your teachers. The experiences you had at school may well have affected your experience of yourself as an agent of action and change. They may well have affected how you see yourself as a person and your beliefs about yourself and the world. There is no excuse for bullying, just as there is no excuse for physical violence. Verbal violence is also very damaging and shows difficulties with learning how to relate to people in a respectful and meaningful way. Bullies may learn by their parents modelling the behaviour, or they may be essentially insecure and see their bullying as a way of making themselves more secure in their relationships with their friends. School is a place where any difference may be noticed and attacked, whether by teasing or bullying. In any case, bullying is not a nice thing to engage in and puts the victim into a negative emotional state.

While it is the case that most schools have anti-bullying programs in place, bullying still may occur online, and this has had dire consequences in some instances. If you are, or have been, a bully then you should think about the consequences of your behaviour on your victims. Think about what would be the effect on you if someone did it to you. Put yourself in your victims' shoes. This is empathy. If you are still engaged in bullying behaviour take steps to stop. There are other ways to feel good about yourself which we will be covering in this book.

If you are a victim of bullying it can be hard not to take what is said to heart, but it is best not believe it. It is, after all, only somebody else's thoughts. It is important that you counteract what is said with positive statements about yourself. It is also important to tell someone, a teacher, employer, family member or friend. They will support you and help you to come up with positive words that will counteract the bullying, as well as helping to address the situation. It is important to believe in yourself and to believe in your positive characteristics as a person, and not to allow the bully to win by believing them. This is not to say that the bullying doesn't hurt – it does – but it is positive to take action by talking about it to the right people and working out how to deal with the hurt, emotionally and psychologically. You can imagine that you are in a bubble of energy that only allows positive things through and deflects negative words and energy. Negativity just bounces off and is reflected back to the source. This is just one way to deal with it. Talk about it so you feel supported. Tell your family, friends, employers, co-workers and teachers. Strategies for dealing with bullying vary from school to school, but if you are getting bullied at work then there are usually processes you can follow to get some redress.

FRIENDSHIPS

We usually become friends with people with whom we have something in common. We stay friends if the common interaction grows into liking and the relationship helps to fulfil our needs of friendship and association. Someone is an acquaintance if they are not well known but you spend some time with them on occasions. With a friend, you can share quite a lot about yourself and they will share themselves too, so that you end up with quite a strong bond. The more time you spend together and the more you share yourself then the more likely it is you have a strong friendship. Of course, it does depend on the personalities of those involved, and that needs to be taken into account in any analysis of the friendship. It is helpful to at least occasionally look at motives and intent for behaviours you observe. In this way you will know them better and you can come to a conclusion, in some form, about your friendship. By observing behaviour it is possible to infer motive and, additionally, you have the luxury of being able to ask your friend what motivated him/her. From this conversation you will come to know your friend better.

To be a good friend it is important to encourage them to achieve their goals, to support them on the way and to lend a sympathetic ear. You don't need to fix their problems, you just need to listen. By all means make a suggestion, but it is your friend's life and only they are responsible for their own life. You can strongly advise your friend to do or not do something that is in their long-term interest, but if they still decide on a certain action then you can't change that. It is helpful to look at long term consequences when making decisions to act in a certain way. Although this is not the first and easiest way of thinking when one is a young adult, it will serve you well if you put it into practice. Ask yourself, 'If I do act, then what are the long-term consequences?' For example, if it involves drinking alcohol then you need to bring into account the effects of binge drinking on your behaviour, your brain and your memory. Then you can ask yourself, 'Does this particular behaviour help me fulfil my values – those of importance to me?' After that you can think about more short and medium-term consequences, such as having fun with your friends. You can also advise your friend to make their decision based along these lines. Whatever decision they ultimately make may be different will be up to them.

The same process can be taken when you feel that you are under pressure to engage in behaviour that might be risky or have negative consequences. Peer pressure can be a very strong force when we are young, because we need to feel that we belong, and in order to belong we think that we need to 'join in' with others. This idea, to some degree, is in our heads. Friends are not necessarily going to drop you just because you don't go along with them on occasion, or engage in a particular behaviour. If they do then you are probably better off without them, and if they don't drop you then you know they are true friends. The important aspect to this is that you are true to yourself and don't get swept up into being someone you don't want to be. Or doing things you don't want to do.

The issue is that these sort of things need to be thought of and decided on before the situation arises, because peer pressure and the heat of the moment can conspire to make you decide in the wrong direction. If you have made a firm decision prior to the occasion and worked out what you will do, then when the occasion arises you will be able to recognise it and take action, whether this means that you leave the situation or try to convince your friends against it. You will know that you have done the right thing by yourself and by society. The question of legalities should also be taken into account when making decisions, not just risk and possible consequences. If it's illegal, the safest option is to not do it, because the consequences might be catastrophic. It is not enough to believe that you are bulletproof or that you won't get caught, or that nothing bad will happen: you aren't bulletproof, you may well get caught, and the law of averages says that bad things do happen. The more that you act within the law the less likely it is that negative consequences will occur.

Laws are made for the wellbeing and smooth running of society. If you don't drink and drive, don't use drugs, and don't drive above the speed limit then you are less likely to have a motorcycle accident, and, therefore, less likely to die or be incapacitated for the rest of your life. This is a fact. More deaths and incapacitation occur for young males between sixteen and twenty-four than any other group. Your body is your temple. It is yours alone. You therefore are in charge of it and have the right to say what you do with it. Because you are on a lifelong journey with it, you need to be aware of the consequences of actions and practices that may have a detrimental effect on your physical body, your psychology, and your sense of self.

It is possible to be part of an unhealthy friendship group. You may recognise this situation by the amount of negative feelings that you experience due to that group. If you feel that you are being taken advantage of, feel that you are being used, that your values are being overridden by what you are doing, or that you just don't want to be a part of what you are doing, then you need to take a step back. If you find yourself in this situation, the best thing you can do is say, 'No' to going out with your friends. Despite the fact that you will feel pressured into going out and doing the things they want to do, it is good in this instance to be strong and not go. The point might be that they are not really your friends, and you may be able to find a better group of friends that will not use and abuse you, or act in ways that are illegal or immoral. It may be tough to say no, but you need to put yourself first.

CLOSE RELATIONSHIPS

Being in a close relationship does not mean that you can't have friends and hobbies outside of that relationship. In fact, it is a good idea to have at least a few things that the two of you don't share. It is better for mental health and overall wellbeing. Then when you do come together for those things you share you will be able to be enthusiastic about them.

In any relationship, communication is the key to success. That means communication both ways. It is best to be honest and up front about everything. While you might share some things about yourself with your friends, you might share everything with your partner, so that they may know you and trust you. The better you know someone the more you are able to trust them. If something happens and that trust is lost then it takes quite a long time to get that trust back again.

It is helpful to communicate assertively, so that both partners know where they stand and may ask for what they want within the relationship and get their needs met. Sometimes it's the case that one partner may be dominant and the other more submissive. This is not always positive for the more submissive partner. It depends on the personalities involved and the behaviours that are involved, as well. The more equal each partner can be in the relationship, the better.

If you are able to talk and communicate your thoughts, feelings and ideas to your partner, and visa versa, then you have a good basis for a relationship.

Every now and then it is a good idea to sit down and discuss how you both see the relationship, and where you see it going. Are you both getting your needs met? Are you both happy? Would you like something to change? Would you like to do more things together, or would you like more time for your own pursuits?

The more honest and open you are the better you will be able to communicate. One difference between males and females seems to be that males are not always comfortable talking about emotions and feelings, whereas females like doing this. If you are male, particularly if you are in a heterosexual relationship, and you like to fix things, then you are just going to have to be OK with listening to your partner talk about feelings. You don't need to fix anything – by listening and responding in the right way you will be helping your partner to feel better. So active listening is a key factor in this process. What active listening involves is essentially repeating some of the words that are stated in a way that affirms the other person. For example, if your partner says they are upset about something, say to them 'you feel upset'. This will indicate to them that you are listening and understand what they are feeling. They will then be able to say more about the situation. They will feel that they are heard. Whether you are in a heterosexual or a same sex relationship, whether you are a man who is comfortable talking about his emotions with a male or female partner who finds it difficult to discuss feelings, or whether neither partner finds emotional conversations easy, these ways of understanding the other person may be helpful. It doesn't matter who the person is who wants to fix stuff, that person needs to pay attention to active listening and help their partner in this process. If both of you are able to active listen to the other then communication will be good.

ACTIVE LISTENING EXERCISE

A. Work is pissing me off. Every time I try to do something right I get criticised. It really upsets me.

B. You feel upset when you get criticised.

A. Yes and I'm not sure how to do it differently.

B. You're unsure what to do.

A. Yes. What might be best?

B. What are your options as you see them?

> In this conversation B is helping A to move forward and process feelings. A gets to the idea of problem solving in a short time as she feels heard and understood.

CONSTRUCTIVE EXERCISES

An exercise that you can do is to count the negative to positive statements that you say to your family members or partner. This ratio is called the Losada ratio and it is an important indicator of the health of the relationship. If it is 3:1 (negative to positive) then you are in trouble. If it's 1:2.9 you are OK, but if it's 1:5 then your relationship is terrific. In counting this ratio it is best to use the unit of sentences and turns in speaking. See *Flourish* (11) for a more in-depth look at this.

One goal that comes out of this, however, is that if you are interested in improving your relationships you need to increase the number of positive statements you speak. This may take some time to manage, but if you go through the process of setting the goal, monitoring your behaviour and putting new behaviours into place as discussed in my previous book, *Setting Yourself Free* (12), then you will be well on your way.

If you have some constructive criticism to tell someone, then the best way to say it is in a sandwich of positive statements. Thus you could say, 'I love the meals you make when it's your turn to cook. It would be great if you could give the kitchen a bit of a clean as you go along, just to keep everything organised, like the helpful way you always write on the kitchen blackboard when we're running out of something.'

This sandwich helps the other person to be buoyed up by the positive statements and although he or she will hear the criticism they are more likely to take it on board because of the way it has been delivered.

MANAGING EXPECTATIONS

In any close relationship sex is an important component. Consent is crucial in any sexual encounter. Between two consenting adults sex can be brilliant. Communication is a key issue here. Negotiating intimate relationships can be difficult, but it can be done. Look at co-dependence and dependency. Make sure that you are not making the other person responsible for your responsibilities. Look at whether you need the other person to be a certain way. If, for instance, a number of your partners have had addiction issues, then you may be co-dependent and trying to rescue them. Change this and find a partner who is different. It is impossible to change people. They have to do it themselves.

Nowadays there is online dating. Expectations here also need to be managed. When you meet people online you may gain an initial perception of them. Communications online can become quite intense. However, this may just be online, and the reality when you meet them may be very different. So you need to keep your feet on the ground and try not to build your expectations up too much. One thing about online dating is that when you do meet them, you may know a bit more about them than most people you meet face-to-face for the first time. Although it might be intense online, when you meet them it might feel quite different. It is also worth keeping in mind that people may not be who they say they are. At the very least, this could lead to disappointment. At the very worst, you could put yourself in danger from scammers or people with violent tendencies. When meeting someone in person that you have met online, always tell someone where you are going and make sure you meet in a public place.

GENERALLY SPEAKING

It's important that you feel in control of yourself. It's even better if you feel that you are in control of your life. You need to be able to feel that you are an agent and have primary effect on things like relationships. If you are always doing what others want then think about what this means for your own behaviour and identity. Perhaps it is OK if you sincerely want to do what others want you to do, but if there are times when you only go along with others because you feel you can't say no then please see the chapter on assertiveness and meeting your needs.

Do you make suggestions about outings, and are they considered? Do you feel that others notice you, care about you and are willing to go along with you? The answers to these questions will show you where you have agency and where improvement could be made. Even though it might not feel like it, one area where you do have agency is in the way that you can change yourself, if you so desire. You can change yourself, but you can't change others. If you change first then others may change their behaviours towards you. Whether or not they do, it is a good idea to focus on self-change, rather than trying to change others.

At times, throughout our relationships, revealing our vulnerable side is a good idea. Showing vulnerability helps others to understand us better and to trust us more. It also means that we become stronger within ourselves. Being vulnerable sometimes shows others, especially our partner, that we trust them. It is most helpful in a heart-to-heart discussion about the relationship. It can help a relationship to grow, and can be used at various times to reveal little known information or secrets about oneself that may be shared in a close relationship.

FROM TEEN TO ADULT

Once you transition from being a teen to a young adult, the expectation of society is that you now have the responsibility for your own behaviour. Behaviour may lead to consequences, and you need to accept these too. Society also expects that you will become a contributing member. So it is at this time, when turning eighteen years old, that you can start to think about behaviour and consequences more than in the past. Many cultures have a rite of passage that marks the transition from childhood to adulthood as its focus. Eighteenth birthday parties probably don't get the idea across.

The way you transition to being an adult is very individual. If you have accepted the idea of responsibility then you are more likely to take yourself and your world a little more seriously than others who have not. It helps to have discussions around what happens in the world, particularly around behaviour and possible consequences. It is, however, the application of this idea to oneself that is important. Some people do not get it, and others get it, but carry on regardless.

It is possible to engage in taking on responsibility in a gradually increasing way. Thus, if you are attending a college or university, you can take on responsibility for your own learning. To achieve this, you would be doing more study, completing the readings, doing the suggested extras and making sure that your assignments are in on time. Where you find work, then you can accept responsibility for your working performance, and can make sure that you are a model employee. Where you can't find work then you can still take responsibility for your search. You can send in applications, ensure they are the best you can make them, do your best at interviews, and generally try hard to find work.

At the same time as you are engaging in these behaviours and taking responsibility for yourself, there is also your social life to consider. Just as with your education and employment, the more responsibility you can apply here, the better. The older you get, the easier it is to see the connection between behaviour and consequences. When you do become more responsible and consider others as well as yourself, then you become a true adult.

SELF-ASSESSMENT

You could carry out a survey of your family and friends and ask them how they would describe you as a person. Write down their responses – don't judge them, but see them as a starting point to a better you. What you are getting is baseline data about how you come across to others. You could also ask your family and friends the questions, 'What do you think would help me to become better?' and, 'How do you think I should change?' If those you ask are answering honestly and sincerely, you should get a result that provides some indication of future goals that you could action and achieve, should you so decide. You then have the choice of working out how you want to be as a person and what identity you project. There are some things that are very difficult to change about ourselves, but it is possible to become better at things such as being assertive, and getting on with people. Additionally, you can improve your skills, and learn new things. As you do these things you also may change your beliefs, values, ideas and attitudes.

BECOMING AWESOME

- Take responsibility for yourself, at school or work, and in your social life.
- Keep your activities on the legal side.

- Make sure that you are treating your body with respect and say no when you want to.
- Be open and honest in your relationships.
- Ask your friends for feedback so you can get some ideas about what you can do to improve yourself and your relationships.
- By taking these steps, your relationships can start becoming awesome.

Chapter 5

Sex and Sexuality

Sexual identity and sexual orientation is innate. That is, you are born that way. Neither of these is open to change (1). You feel you are a male or female, and you are attracted to males or females, or both. In the womb, nature may take a bit of an unsual turn and so you might end up being physically a different sex to how you feel. Nature produces a mix of sexual identities and orientations, and we need to see all these differences as natural, because they are. Where there are differences that an individual can change to enhance his or her life, then this change is appropriate.

Sexual preferences are laid down in late childhood, up to the time when puberty kicks in. Preferences revolve around orientation. You might like bums, breasts and so on. When the preference focuses on usual aspects, then that is considered 'normal'. When the preference is unusual, such as in age, situations or objects, then it is called a fetish. Once formed, preferences endure (1).

COMING OUT

Children easily identify what is accepted as 'normal' in society. Because the predominant story is straight and heterosexual, difference is not always accepted by everyone. It is usual for those children who do not fit the 'norm' to feel that they are different when quite young. Consciously identifying where you fit in may not always occur as a teen, but because sexual identity is now becoming more fluid for young people, and is becoming more accepted in many societies, then hopefully more timely 'coming outs' may happen. Working out your sexual identity, from childhood up, can be a time of inner turmoil and conflict. There may be bullying and problems at school. The internet is not far away, and you will find 'coming out' stories on there, so that you will not feel so isolated. Since this time is so confusing and full of conflict for some people, the rates of suicide and attempts at suicide are higher than average for this group. You are not alone. Attempting suicide is not the answer, but talking to someone is. Ask for help. This is a good time to seek some counselling so that you can make sense of your situation and make plans for managing it. There are telephone counselling services available, or you may find a counsellor in your area that you can see face-to-face. See (2) for more information.

It is helpful to be able to come out to your family and friends at a time that is appropriate for you. It is important to be able to understand how your family may react and to prepare yourself for that reaction. It is to be hoped that your family are supportive and accept you as you are. And, of course, your friends too. You may tell those people that are more likely to support you first. You may also consider how much you accept yourself as a sexual being having the identity and orientation that you have. The more comfortable you are with the situation the better able you will be to withstand any ensuing conflict. This might mean that you sit with the idea for a little while before you start coming out to others. Or perhaps only tell a select few.

TRANSGENDER

For transgender kids the situation in Australia is becoming better than it was. Provided the situation is picked up before puberty, hormone blockers can be prescribed so that puberty is delayed. The assessment of two psychiatrists is required for hormone treatment and gender reassignment to take place. Recently, a full sitting of the Family Court made a ruling that the court is no longer involved in the process granting young transgender kids experiencing gender dysphoria the right to gender-affirming hormone treatment. This situation will make it a less costly and a more humane process of transitioning for young people.

It is important for you to accept your own sexuality as well as that of others. It is who you are deep down, and requires acceptance. And if you accept your own sexuality then others have the right that you accept theirs too.

CONSENT

No-one has the right to abuse you. No-one has the right to do anything that you do not consent to. Consent is a very important aspect of any type of sexual behaviour. Whether you are male or female you need to gain verbal consent to whatever you are intending to do with a partner. And if at any stage you get a 'no' or any word or behaviour that might indicate a negative then you need to stop, immediately, what you are doing. It doesn't matter if you got a verbal agreement previously or not. It is important to take notice of the change of agreement, because legally you have no leg to stand on if you continue and, even more importantly, you are violating your partner's right as a person and human being. You would like your rights to be respected, so ensure that you also afford those rights to others. The legal age of consent in South Australia is seventeen years old. Legally, anyone under that age cannot give consent. You are liable to be charged and convicted of sexual intercourse without consent of a minor if you have sex with a minor.

If your partner is over seventeen but doesn't consent to a sexual act then you can be charged for similar offences. Such a charge and conviction may blight your life forevermore. So think of the long-term consequences and respect the rights of others, as well as sticking to the consent rules, and you will not get into trouble with the law.

Only you have the right to allow or prohibit behaviours that involve you and your body. This includes sexting. You need to be aware that others are not necessarily to be trusted with your images and they may well end up in the online sphere. Once images are on the internet it is very difficult to get them off. One policy to look at taking is to not send any images anywhere, even if you think it would be a fun thing to do. Better to have a face-to-face exchange rather than using your phone.

Consent in any sexual encounter is crucial. You can withdraw consent at any time too. If your partner respects you then they will stop. If they don't stop they can be charged with rape or sexual assault. Between two consenting adults sex can be brilliant. It can be inspiring, rejuvenating and satisfying. Where love is involved sex is much better than if you just like someone. In any case, it is important to think about any possible consequences of your behaviour. Birth control needs to be discussed with your partner, and the use of condoms is a good idea. Condoms stop the transmission of sexually transmitted diseases such as Chlamydia, which can make females infertile. Syphilis and gonorrhoea are also possible sexually transmitted diseases that can be very unpleasant, although nowadays they are treatable with penicillin. Another STD to be aware of is HIV (Human Immunodeficiency Virus), which can have life-long repercussions. Although the first three mentioned STDs are becoming more prevalent, HIV should be considered to be possible. The safest way to treat a new partner is to use condoms until you are both tested for STDs. And then you can continue to use condoms or use the pill or other IOD device. If your male partner complains that he doesn't like using condoms because the feeling is more limited, the answer to this is that they will last longer and get more satisfaction in knowing they are satisfying you.

If you are male, you need to have some say in birth control too. It might be important to use condoms if you think your partner is not on the pill so you will not be an unexpected father. It is much better for children to be planned by both parents, who have discussed everything together. If you want a child and you are quite young think about what this might mean for your life. Work out if it is the right time or whether waiting a couple of years might be better. It's much better to plan and to discuss with your partner, because they are involved, whether you like it or not.

HEALTHY SEXUAL RELATIONSHIPS

In a healthy sexual relationship you can keep safe boundaries between fantasy and reality. Any fantasies that you indulge in when you are masturbating are best kept to those times. If you find you need to fantasise when you are making love with a partner, then recognise it for what it is; just a fantasy. Any games that you play together should stay in that realm of fantasy. Theoretically, it should be possible to just focus on the physical sensations that you are experiencing and orgasm from the pleasure of your sexual encounter.

Most of all, if you have a healthy relationship, you are having fun. When you are fulfilling your lust with someone you love, then you make a deep emotional connection with them. It is extremely satisfying and life affirming.

It may be a good idea to sit down and define to at least yourself, if not with your partner, where your boundaries are in relation to sex. This will be related to what you like and dislike, and what you are willing to give and receive. Define your boundaries and it will be easier for you to recognise when those boundaries are being crossed and you are being taken advantage of. You could also have a conversation with your partner and define the boundaries, and talk about your partner's boundaries too. Once you have both talked about the activities you like and dislike then you will be on the same page, and your sex life may improve.

In a healthy sexual relationship sex is only a part of the relationship. You need to enjoy each other's company, and spend time together doing things you both like. You can also socialise together, in a group with others or just the two of you. A big part of the relationship should be communication. Communication is the key to a healthy relationship, since you need to understand each other, and you do this through healthy communication, in whatever mode this is. See the previous chapter for more information.

UNHEALTHY RELATIONSHIPS

How do you recognise an unhealthy relationship? A relationship is unhealthy when one person feels that they are being taken advantage of, when their personal boundaries are being crossed, and when they feel used and abused. An unhealthy relationship exists when there is violence, but the abuse can also be psychological. When you are being controlled by your partner, when you do not have the freedom to be yourself, when sex is the primary activity, when you are being criticised all the time and being put down in front of others and even when the two of you are alone, these are all indications that should make you think about whether you want to remain in such a relationship. While some of these situations may be easier to manage than others, they are all signs of at least a slightly unhealthy situation. You are, after all, two different people in a relationship and you should each accept the other as an individual person who is different to yourself. There is an intersection where the two of you meet, and that is you as a couple. This is where you communicate, agree to decisions, talk together, and do things together. But apart from the two of you as a couple you are two unique individuals, and respect for each other should be paramount. This should be shown by respecting each other's personal boundaries. Situations like the ones discussed here actually break personal boundaries.

Sex and power are interrelated. If you feel that your relationship has an unequal balance in favour of one person, then explore what this means and think about whether it is really about power. Some people exploit others, and feeling or being the more powerful one in the relationship may be a buzz for them. This is also an unhealthy relationship. It may be important to get out when you can.

How to leave an unhealthy relationship may be problematic. It may be that it is not easy to leave someone, due to all the things you have together, whether memories, possessions, and history. If you still love them, then you could give them the opportunity to change their behaviour and have some relationship counselling. Whether this would work is a debatable issue. However, it might. If it does, then that is great. Otherwise, and certainly if you have in the past asked them to change their behaviour but they haven't, then leaving may be the best option. You don't want to put up with more years of having your personal boundaries crossed and feeling the same as you have been. It may be helpful to engage in individual counselling so that you can gather your resources together and make plans for the future. It will be an ego strengthening exercise to do so. If you are not married then you can organise a cleaner break than if you are married. However, how you leave is going to be dependent on your partner's reaction to the suggestion of your leaving.

You could check out the legal situation, and also check the shelters in your area if you are going to need one. Preparation is a good thing. Plan the easiest way of leaving. Discussion is preferable, but may not always be advisable or appropriate. You might need to find other accommodation. Moving out your possessions will also be necessary. It is easier if you can move out, rather than getting your partner to move out. But each situation is unique and will depend upon circumstances.

Organisation will help.

HISTORICAL SEXUAL ABUSE

If you have suffered historical sexual abuse it will be necessary for you to redefine yourself. You can choose to be a survivor rather than a victim. If you continually bring the subject up, particularly in context of being unable to achieve things you would like to achieve, you may be defining yourself as a victim. Choose instead to be a survivor who has healthy boundaries. So set a boundary for others to show respect to you. Do not let others take advantage of you, but speak out when you notice this happening. Be assertive. Set boundaries that allow you to care for yourself. Do things to nurture yourself on a regular basis. Let others know when they are abusing your boundaries, and give them consequences for crossing them. It might be three different actions that you tell them you will put into place. You can create your own consequences, but you need to tell them what will happen. Thus you need to be assertive. See the chapter on assertiveness for further information.

BECOMING AWESOME

- Communicate with your family, and ask for help if you need it.
- Communicate with your partner and ensure consent in any sexual act.
- Have healthy relationships with others and recognise when you are in an unhealthy relationship. Leaving may be the best option in the latter case.
- Accept both your own and others' sexuality.
- By taking these steps you can start creating an awesome attitude to sex.

Chapter 6

Interests and Hobbies

Hobbies and interests have a role in life to allow you to find yourself and to express yourself. This helps you to gain a more complete image of yourself as a human being, and in the process you may find many benefits. What you may get out of them may be separate from what you get out of other parts of life. If you try a particular activity and find that you really like it then you can continue with it. Otherwise, you can try something else. Hobbies are individually unique in enjoyment and talent-discovery ability. So it is a matter of thinking you might be interested or knowing that you are, trying it and testing to see whether the interest holds or not. Based on this you can make the correct decision about whether it is right for you. Where you find you have a talent for something then this may be a bonus. You can then continue the activity or take it further, if that's what you want to do.

Even if you don't stand out from the crowd in terms of talent you can still improve your skill level in whatever activity you do. It is said that it takes 10,000 hours of practice to become a top performer. To hone skills and be the best you can is a worthwhile goal. However, it depends on your mindset and, ultimately, on what you want to achieve with your activity.

POSITIVE EFFECTS

Where you are passionate about your hobby or interest and you are able to engage in it then this has positive repercussions. You feel good when you engage in it and this feeds positive self-esteem, self-confidence, and feelings of self-competence, and is likely to give you transferable skills to take out into the wider world. Transferable skills are things that you accumulate that are useful in all areas of life, and across many different situations. These may include such things as attention to detail, concentration and focus, organisational skills, leadership ability, strong teamwork, communication skills, knowledge, and strategic ability. Then there are the specific skills that are related to the particular hobby or interest. You may become fit and healthy too, which will stand you in good stead. Transferable skills may help you secure a place at university, where you may have gained knowledge and interview skills through school and your hobbies. This might help to define what you want to do.

A hobby may also be an addition in your life, or it might build on what you are already doing so that it adds to an existing framework. This situation may mean that you are being aided in your craft by what you are doing as a hobby.

When others are involved then it gives you team skills as well. Friends and like-minded people are an added bonus. If your hobby is an extra-curricular interest then you may have the opportunity to gain skills that you may not otherwise learn. Becoming involved in something outside of your family and school means that you become a more multidimensional person.

MORE BENEFITS

A hobby or interest may lead to a career or future career opportunities. It is totally up to you how you engage in your hobby. It can be a lifelong interest which you engage with in your leisure time, you may just do it for a period of time, or it can turn into a career. If you have a talent for it and you are passionate about it then it may indicate a positive career move. However, having a talent does not need to define you. It is totally your choice as to whether you follow a path that involves your talent. It is your life and your choice.

By engaging in a hobby that holds your interest, you are expressing who you are. This has positive health benefits; not only for physical health, but for mental health as well. You may find a sense of freedom in engaging in your hobby or activity and find that time just flies by. This is the space of being 'In Flow', when you are absolutely present in the now and you are engaging in what you love. This is what you are looking for when you are engaging in your hobby, and this space can inform your decisions.

SOME NEGATIVE SITUATIONS

When you are forced to engage in a hobby or activity you find you don't like then this has negative consequences. You end up resenting the time spent, resenting whoever is enforcing the activity, and it's likely to put you off it for quite some time. It is only when you also choose to do it that the negatives won't outweigh the positives.

It's possible to have unfulfilled desires of engaging in activities due to circumstances. Perhaps the costs were prohibitive or somehow you were unable to engage in your interests. If this happened when you were young then where you still have those desires as an adult, you can choose to set a goal and go about achieving it. It is never too late to try. The circumstances need to come together so that everything is in place for you to reach your goal. On occasion, the possibilities may not be present and the time for your desired outcome may have passed. You may be able to find a possible alternative activity that fulfils at least a part of your unfulfilled desires if this is the case. There may be other ways that you can be fulfilled in your interest area. For example, if you are too old to reach competition level in dance or sport, then it might be possible to become a coach or teacher.

Similarly, where you were not supported in your desire to engage in a hobby or interest then this may have had a great impact on you. It may mean that you needed to come up with other alternatives that may have been supported and these may not have been as close to your heart. It depends on individual circumstances and the activity whether it can be picked up later in life. Again, you can find ways of fulfilling your interest by perhaps getting into an ancillary role or becoming a coach or teacher.

START OUT EARLY

While young, it's a good idea to find out what interests you. Try as many things that might be hobbies or sporting interests as you can. Hopefully, your parents helped you and guided you in attending classes, games, and so on, and let you follow your interests and passions. Depending on what it is and how skilled you become at it, it may become an even bigger part of your life. So think about the hobbies you had as a child and while growing up. Whatever you did may have helped you sort out what you like and what you aren't really interested in. The question then becomes what are you still involved in? Have some interests lasted and how do you feel about them?

Hopefully, reading books is on your list of hobbies and interests. Reading books helps you learn about the world, increases your vocabulary, and usually helps spelling too. And, of course, it is a fun thing to do. If books are interesting for you then there are a number of areas you could take this. You could join a book club, learn about particular subjects and topics, or learn about various countries before you go travelling.

SELF-ASSESSMENT

You can make a list of all the things you have tried, and note which ones you are still continuing, and which ones you love to do. If you have a natural talent in what you love then make a note of this too. This is important and may well indicate a possible career path.

Interests and hobbies may change as you grow older. Interests are not necessarily fixed at any age. Because interests change over time you can become more fulfilled by engaging in hobbies and activities that are appropriate at the time.

It is a great idea to be involved in sporting activities while young, and later in life. It is a good source of exercise, and if it's a team sport then you learn how to cooperate and be a team player. Even if you are only involved for a few years you will gain benefits. Trying things out is good, and if you find you have a natural talent then this is a bonus. You can then take it further if you are so inclined. You would need to make a decision in consultation with your family as to whether to take your talent further. If you did this and your family helps you then you may be on the way to playing for your team, club, state or even your country. It takes quite a lot of effort and sacrifice to do this, but can be extremely rewarding.

Sometimes you may gain recognition by engaging in your hobby or interest. It is a good idea to see any recognition gained as a bonus, rather than expecting this as a primary goal. It isn't only sport in which you might gain recognition. There are other activities you can engage in such as chess, debating, art, music or any number of things. It's really a matter of testing yourself to see where your interests lie, and perhaps taking it as far as you can. It will depend on where you want to go in life and whether you believe in yourself and your talents. It also depends on your family and whether they have been encouraging you to follow what you are good at. Sometimes family can be a positive influence, and sometimes they can be a negative influence. Sometimes you might make the wrong decision and sometimes you might make the correct decision.

NEW DIRECTIONS

When you are willing to try new activities you are steering yourself into new directions. The outcome is unknown and you are spreading your sphere of influence. It doesn't really matter what the ultimate outcome or result will be, because the process of engaging in it is what counts. The process is likely to open up skill enhancement and learnings that will be of benefit to you. New learnings create new pathways in your brain and this all goes towards your growth as a person. So whether you take it a lot further or whether you don't, the process is important. Nothing you learn is ever wasted, as it all goes towards becoming part of who you are. Follow your enthusiasm and you will find whatever you are interested in. Taking the time to consolidate is also helpful in the learning process. Allow yourself to plateau for a while as you practice what you have learnt. Then the new behaviours will become a more intrinsic part of you; they will become automatic. The new thinking will become more familiar and you'll be able to engage in the activity as you would wish.

EXPLORING TALENTS

If you have found throughout your childhood that you are creative in some way then you should nurture this creativity. Where you are artistic and can draw then this might pave your way into some type of employment where it is helpful to be able to draw. Think about graphic design, architecture, cartoonist or artist, for a start. Be creative in your thinking. Where is your passion, and your love? Follow it. If you are creative in any way then you can carry this into a myriad of hobbies as well as working roles. Think big.

Where you have a talent for music and have had lessons as a child then think about whether you want to continue this now, and what form it should take. Brainstorm some ideas. You could be involved in the music industry in some way – there are many different jobs here. Do you want to play music in a band, for example, or do you just like being around musicians and can see yourself involved in an ancillary position? Investigate where you have a talent or desire. Where you enjoy performing for others then think about the setting you would prefer, whether theatre, film, or TV. If this type of environment excites you then think about what you would like to do in that environment and whether it would be a career or something you do as an interest. Perhaps you like performing but are also passionate about what is happening. In this case maybe journalism would be suitable.

Where you have been interested in dance and movement when younger, the question becomes would you like to continue this as an adult? If you are also able to sing in tune then this might indicate some performing role that may be a career option. It might be worthwhile to continue and see where it might take you. It depends on your talents and how much effort you put into it, as well as a degree of luck. Where is your passion? What do you love to do? It is important to work this out so that you can make a decision about your life. The more you brainstorm ideas and think outside the box, the better.

If you have a sporting talent you could consider where you'd like to take this. You don't have to take it up as a career. You could consider a supporting role. Or even just keep it at a local level and play your games on the weekends. As with any talent, you don't need to pursue it as a career. Consider what you want to gain from your hobby. Think long term as well as medium term.

Often, it might be good to train in something that could be a fallback position if your first love doesn't work out. This would also be helpful in the situation of being able to find employment while enhancing your performing career, for example. So think about what you could bear to do while you are working on your dream. It's always helpful to have a plan B and it will make you more employable in the long run.

TRAVEL

It is educational to travel and find out about how other people live, survive and thrive in other countries and cultures. Travelling during your gap year can be a great opportunity to begin exploring the world. Being aware of the risks and dangers in the places you want to visit is important, and you may wish to confine yourself to visiting those places that are low risk. Discuss travelling with your family and your friends, and you might find that you have a friend who would like to travel with you. There is, to some extent, safety in numbers, and it is easier if you have someone with you to discuss situations that come up. Travel advisories are on the Australian Government website (1). You don't have to travel in your gap year. You may prefer to find work or volunteer with a charity.

Make sure that you learn about the countries you are going to before you travel. Read about the culture and customs. Then you will not be caught out in a situation where you get frowned upon, or even possibly find yourself in gaol. When you travel, tell people where you are going and develop strategies to keep yourself safe wherever you go.

You can make a contribution to local communities at the same time as travelling. Some ways of doing this may be good and others dubious. Make sure that you do your research before you go, and investigate properly so that you engage with the good organisations that help you contribute locally. There are many options, from becoming an eco-tourist to volunteering on building projects abroad. Take the time to explore different options so that you can find your idea of a good time, whether you are helping others or not.

There are different ways of travelling and working around the world. Ensure that you have the correct visa for the particular country you are visiting, and that you fulfil the criteria that the country has for such visas. It is beneficial to use what you have to explore the world around you.

GENERAL

Hobbies and interests can continue over a lifetime. There may be something that you like to do when you have some free time. You may set aside some time every week to walk, hike, or cycle. It doesn't matter if an interest just remains something that you do regularly. That is fine. There is no rule that says something you like needs to become a career. Sometimes it can. Otherwise it just stays as an interest. It is helpful to have hobbies and interests. They provide rest, relaxation, and exercise, and can be very beneficial to your heath overall. Hobbies and interests are certainly good for your mental health. Whether it is something that you do by yourself or with others, such activities provide time for you. If you can look after yourself then this means you are more capable of looking after others too. Engaging in hobbies and interesting activity refreshes your mind and helps you to gain a new perspective on life. Engaging in hobbies is where you find your freedom and fulfil yourself, and presents the opportunity to feed and nurture yourself. Spend time on things that you like to do whenever you are able. You will be glad when you do.

BECOMING AWESOME

- Explore a variety of interests and hobbies and find the ones that you enjoy.
- Think about whether your hobbies and interests might lead to possible career options or whether they can remain lifelong activities.
- Plan some time to spend on your interests during the week. It helps rest and relaxation as well as charging your batteries.
- Think about expressing this talent throughout your life in a way that is enhancing for you and your life.
- By taking these steps, you will be on your way to having awesome interests and hobbies.

Chapter 7

Finances

Given how our society and the world economy is organised we need to accept that money is necessary. We need money to survive. So what can you do to arrange your finances in a way that is helpful to you? Money is both symbolic and physical, but is also on another level, energy.

There are some ideas around that look at the relationship individuals have with money. Thus the beliefs you have and attitudes that you have towards money may affect to a large extent, the experience you have with money in your life (1). For instance if you have a scarcity mentality then you may be forever chasing it. Whereas if you have an abundance mentality then you may be fine. There is probably a balance here. If you believe that you will be financially comfortable then you may find that you are more able to live within your means. After all, all you need is more money coming in than going out. You may need some self-discipline, but it will be worth it in the long run.

BUDGETING

A budget is an important feature of your financial arrangements particularly if you have a limited income. It can help you to apportion your money to the crucial expenses and help you to manage your money overall. Everyone has expenses. As well as outgoings, you hopefully also have some money coming in. It is important to make an account of your money. As part of this process you need to write down all your incoming and outgoing items as they happen. You might have an online accounts ledger or you could buy a journal from a stationery shop and use that. The best journal would be one that has four columns across the page. There is a small column for the date, a larger one for the description, then two smaller columns for income and expenses. As you go through the month you can write down each transaction. At the end of the month you can then total both columns and find out whether you've spent more than you've received (in the red) or if you've received more than you've spent (in the black).

If you write everything down then after a few months you can figure out how much you are spending on average per month. Additionally, you will know what your biggest expenditures are, and you can then look at how you might reduce your spending so that you can save more. It is good if you can save some money. It might be helpful if you can save at least $2,500.00, so that you have some money in case of emergencies.

After you have worked out your average spending, you can make a list of your wants and needs. In the 'needs' column you would have things like rent, food, bills. In the 'wants' column you would probably have things like the money you spend on socialising, and other things you like but don't really need. In this way you can assess where your budget is up to, and whether you are able to save money by perhaps cutting out some of the spending on things you want rather than need.

Nowadays, it is important to have a smart phone. Before you buy a new one, check out whether it is cheaper to buy the phone outright and then buy a plan, rather than paying for it as you go. It is likely that buying outright saves you some money. It is a good idea to investigate phone plans and try to get the cheapest you can for the data and options you want. The more money you can save, the better off you will be in the long run. You will probably have at least a monthly phone bill that you need to take into account in your budget.

From whatever income you get you need to set aside a certain amount for living expenses. The most important of these is your rent or housing, followed by what you spend on food, followed by your phone, then other bills such as gas and electricity, followed by your means of transport, whether a car or bus pass. After all this you need to provide for other expenses that you might pay in cash or on Eftpos, such as for socialising. On a smart phone or Android there are a number of budget apps available that you can use.

Investigate them and choose the best one for you.

SOCIAL SECURITY

It is difficult to afford all these things if you are on Social Security payments and you probably have to rely on savings, if you have any. If you are on Social Security payments and can keep within that limit, so that you don't spend more than you get, you may be making a number of sacrifices. Investigate charity options in your area that may be able to help you manage better.

LIMITED BUDGET

If you are employed, full-time or part-time, then you are possibly in better shape than being unemployed. It is still a really good idea to set a budget and stick with it, but you may be able to save some money so that you can have a better life. Where you have a limited budget it's a good idea to watch debt. It can be more affordable to pay bills monthly rather than yearly, for example car registration and insurance. There may be a facility to enable gas and electricity bills to be paid monthly too. Investigate options such as these, and if they work for you then you can set them up.

CREDIT CARDS

Credit card debt can mount up quickly if you are not paying it off regularly. It is a good policy to only have one credit card. You should investigate the best possible interest charged, and choose the lowest interest with an interest-free period. If you are able to pay off what you owe every month during the interest-free period then you will save yourself a lot of money in the long run. When searching for credit card providers don't be sucked in by interest-free periods on balances switched over. Look more at what the usual interest rate is. It is a false economy to switch over for the sake of switching. Any new purchases will be charged at the going interest rate for that card. If you aren't going to be strict with yourself and just pay off the remaining balance in the next six or twelve months allotted without spending more money on your card then it will cost you a lot more. By reigning in your spending and being strict with yourself, you can get your credit card debt down to zero. Get the number of credit cards you have down to one, and pay it off monthly. Then you will be able to say that you are in control of your credit card rather than letting your spending control you. Additionally, you could have a decision-making period involving your credit card so that you don't just make an impulsive purchase with it. You could for instance leave your credit card in a tub of water in the freezer, so that the ice would need to melt before you can use it at a shop. Perhaps you could also have a policy of saying, 'No' to telemarketers who pressure you to give money to charities. You could also work out for yourself a decision-making routine around online shopping where you use your credit card.

You may need to write a letter to the credit card authorities and state that you want to close your credit card account. Do not get sucked in when they counter with higher limits or less interest or any other ploy. Stick to your goal and remain on track so that you can close the account properly. Do not just cut up your card, because payments may continue to accrue. You need to stop any regular payments that go onto your credit card before you close the account. Get the balance down to zero and then close the account through the bank or other authority. Then do the same with your other credit cards, until you are left with only one. The credit card you keep should have the lowest interest rate with an interest-free period. Then you will need to keep an account of what you put on it so that you can afford to pay it off every month in total. In this way, you will be on top of your spending. Don't forget that the money that you put on your credit card is money you don't have.

SUPERANNUATION

If you are employed then it is worthwhile contributing to your superannuation account. From the financial year 2017/2018, if you contribute to your super and earn less than $51,000 per annum the Australian Government will also contribute an amount of 50% to your super. (check out the situation in your area). It is even more economical and helpful in the long-term to make your own contributions to your super. It helps to consolidate your super money so that it is all in one place, and to do so in an industry super fund. Investigate your industry super fund, especially in terms of fees and insurance. You can organise to have WorkCover and accident insurance as well. Compare fees with MySuper Fund, which is the Australian Government's website. It may be better to nominate the super fund you want your employer to contribute to on your behalf. Then you don't have to keep on rolling small balances over in the future. Contribute to super as and when you can. Do not put it off, because if you do you may regret it later. You will need a lot of money in your super account so that you are able to live comfortably in your retirement. Life can be unpredictable, but it is best to plan for your future, whatever that may look like. For this you need a nest egg.

In the circumstance where you are contributing to your super and generally paying your way in the world then you could think about saving some money towards future investments in your life. Banks and building societies usually have online savings accounts that attract a higher interest rate than everyday accounts. You could save a certain amount each week or fortnight into one of these accounts.

SAVING MONEY

If you have a dedicated account for your savings it will be easier to prove that you have a good savings history. This is what you need when buying a house. See if you can save as quickly as possible. Of course, it will depend on your income and any current expenses that you need to account for. You might need to sacrifice some nights out on the town in order to save faster. It may be worthwhile to do this, though. You could try going out with your friends to places that are less expensive or even free, such as going to the beach or to a park. Another less expensive option is to socialise at your friend's homes, and share the cost of food and drink. It is far cheaper than going out. It is all a matter of negotiation and creativity. Going out and socialising doesn't always have to entail consuming large amounts of alcohol, getting drunk, and spending lots of money.

HOME OWNERSHIP

Since the price of a house in today's market is twelve times the average salary it is much more difficult for first-time home buyers to afford. Paying rent, however, is an expense that is not flowing into an asset; it is something that just needs to be paid to keep a roof over your head. The private rental market is quite expensive, and in order to have a fairly decent place it is hard to save a reasonable amount towards your own home. Two salaries may work better together in this respect, but it is a good idea to come to an arrangement about how you split or join your money.

Where you are still living with your parents, you have a better deal. This is your best opportunity to save money. If you have enough savings it may be more beneficial to purchase an investment property, and when you have enough equity (enough ownership of the property), use this value to purchase your own home. Depending on the property market and the location, some young people discipline themselves to less partying and put their money to good debt. Owning your own home is not good debt. Investment that earns income is good debt. An example of another good debt is an investment portfolio. It doesn't have to be large and it can be added to as you receive a tax refund or a windfall. Another idea is to have one or both of your parents help with either gifted funds or equity in their home or investment property to help you get into the property market, if they are in a positive financial position to do so. Organising a reliable accountant is always worthwhile before entering into investment strategies. Be aware of

Capital Gains Tax and ask questions. Always ask questions.

How you can afford to buy your own home will depend a great deal on your marital status, whether you have a partner or not, and any combined income. Where you have well-paid employment you have a better chance of getting into the housing market earlier. Do a realistic assessment of your ability to buy a house as you go through your life. Explore all options that are available for you to get onto the housing ladder. When the timing is right and you can afford it, then you can achieve your dream.

GOAL SETTING

If you don't have any long-range plans then you are likely to just stay in the same situation, going from week to week. This way will not get you anywhere. It is helpful to set yourself some short, medium and long term goals in a number of areas of life. You could have a career goal, a relationship goal, and a savings goal. Your goal may be to eventually buy a house. This would certainly be a long-term goal, and you could set yourself up with a savings plan as previously discussed. If you have at least two long-term goals, and ensure that you are taking action to achieve them, you will find that you make progress towards your goals. It is important to take a long-term view and to reflect every now and then on your progress, so that you may make changes to your goal, your strategies or the actions that you are taking.

Short and medium-term goals are also good to have, because then you will feel that you are making progress as you achieve them. If you have a savings plan then you could set some short term goals of saving $500, then $1,000, and so on, so the amount of time between achieving your short term goals is not so great, and you feel as though you are getting somewhere. You could then set a goal of $5,000 and then $10,000. These would be medium-term goals. However, achieving them will motivate you to keep on going to your long-term goal. For more on goal setting you can download my chapter on goal setting from my first book, *Setting Yourself Free* (2).

UNEMPLOYMENT

Where you are unemployed then you are likely to be living hand-to-mouth, and the only long-term goal you can think about is to find employment of whatever kind possible, but preferably in an area where you have experience or interest. It's very tough being unemployed, no matter when this occurs in your life. It is particularly demoralising when no-one will even give you a start to show them what you can do. So if your money is low it is good to preserve it as much as possible, rather than spending what you don't have. There are a number of traps for the consumer that you need to be aware of. Firstly, there are advertisements on television for companies that allow you to borrow small amounts of money. These are generally called pay-day loan companies. It is not a good idea to get caught in their clutches. The interest rates they charge are beyond comprehension

(47.8% to 65.3%) and you might end up getting multiple loans to pay off previous loans. For instance, if you were to borrow $300.00 with these interest rates, you would be paying back $443.40 to $579.00. Even if you are optimistic and believe that you can pay the first loan back without any trouble, circumstances may intervene and mean that you get caught up in the treadmill of multiple loans. The majority of people who use pay-day loan companies take out multiple loans. As with any loan, it is important that you do your research and find out the interest rates. Don't just accept that you will be able to afford the repayments. Pay-day loan companies do not stipulate the number of months or years the loan will run for. It is advisable to avoid these companies. The same applies to loan sharks.

There are also companies that offer personal loans. Again, do your research. Check the interest rate, and work out how much money you'd be paying back overall. Ensure that you are getting the best deal if you are after a personal loan. Shop around for the best deal.

Think about credit unions as well as the usual banks. Question yourself whether you really need a personal loan? You may be better off saving up the money. Perhaps you can delay what you want to do with the money. Look at your circumstances properly.

BUYING A CAR

If you are buying a car, the best thing to do is to get organised and find out about getting a car loan from a bank or credit union before you go and sign an agreement for finance at the car yard. If you do organise the loan beforehand, then you will find that you save a great amount of money. The finance companies associated with car yards usually have an interest rate of over 20%. Through a bank you may be able to get a much lower interest rate (perhaps 9% or thereabouts) and for a credit union it would be even lower.

MICROFINANCE

When you need to have an injection of money for any good reason and you are on Social Security payments or have a limited income, then you could try searching for an ethical and secure microfinance company. You may have one in your area. They provide interest-free loans for good reasons. For example, if your refrigerator breaks down or if you need to fix your car, you may be eligible. Do your research and give them a call. They may also have other services available such as saving plans (3).

RENTING

By the same token, stay away from companies that rent out furniture and household items. It is cheaper to shop at second-hand stores or apply to charities for help with furniture and other items they carry.

Renting any household item, no matter what it is, is going to be a lot more expensive than just buying it outright in the first instance. If you were to rent then over the life of the rental agreement you would be likely to pay double or even triple the cost of the items at a normal retail shop. Don't get sucked in by the cheap weekly payments – they go on for too long, and you end up paying far more than the items are worth.

Approach charities in your area and you will get good and useful furniture. You can also look in online groups such as Freecycle + Trash nothing! where people give away furniture and items they no longer want or need. These things may not necessarily be fashionable, but they will still be useful. If you need to move and can't afford the removalist costs then you may be able to approach an organisation such as the Salvation Army for help. For example, if you have been living in South Australia for over five years and are in restricted circumstances, the Salvation Army may be able to help. You may be able to find something similar in your area.

SAVING MONEY

As well as looking at alternatives in areas such as your social life, where you may cut down on going out or choose less expensive places to go, there are a number of other areas you can save money. For example; clothing and lifestyle. Fashion is not the be all and end all. Just because something is fashionable doesn't mean that you need it. This applies not only to clothes, but also to household items and interior decor. You can save a lot of money if you are able to stay off the fashion treadmill. What does it matter if you aren't seen to be particularly fashionable? There are deeper things to be concerned about. You don't need to keep up with the Joneses, Smiths or anyone else. Don't let fashion rule your beliefs and ideas about peoples' worth and value. There are many more values to be concerned about, such as friendship, inclusion, love, truthfulness and respect. Just as long as you wear what you like and it is appropriate for what you need to do in your day-to-day life, and just as long as household items work and are useful, that is all that matters. When it comes down to it, what others think is none of your business. Just as long as *you're* happy, it is fine. Save yourself money and go for comfort and usefulness.

Every area of the media is bombarding you with advertisements on how to live your life. You are never going to achieve it if you believe all you see and hear. Because we live in a throwaway culture, op (opportunity) shop and second-hand furniture provide some great bargains. You can express yourself just as well, and often even more uniquely, through recycling, and upcycling. See it as a way of showing your creativity. Make it something fun. You don't have to spend a lot of money. You can still be stylish, chic, and express yourself on a lower budget.

INSURANCE

When you are looking for an insurance product do some investigation rather than just phoning up a company that advertises on television. Make a list of your own and ring around, asking questions that may sort out which will be the best for you. The importance of doing your own research cannot be underestimated. Google different companies and explore the sites, so that you know you are finding out a wide range of the product you are after. Look at the fine print to see what the terms and conditions are, and talk to people who know the industry. Talk to a number of people before making up your mind. It might be helpful to speak to a financial planner too. Be careful of loopholes and kickbacks in the insurance industry.

Life insurance is probably a good thing to have, so that your family is looked after financially if something happens to you. Compare products and choose the company that offers the best terms and conditions along with a reasonable costing. House and contents insurance is also a good thing to have, so that you are covered if something happens. Make sure you know the circumstances that are covered. For example, it would be helpful if the company covered 'water events' rather than just 'flooding'. This would mean that something like a burst water main causing damage would give you a payout, rather than just a natural disaster. Income protection is the number one personal protection insurance that you should consider to protect your income if fully employed. The contributions are usually tax deductible. Then there is trauma cover, also known as critical-illness cover, which is the cover that most people don't know much about. Trauma cover provides cover if you are diagnosed with a specified illness or injury, such as cancer or a stroke, and may have a big impact on your life. Ask questions and have a meeting with a financial adviser. It is free if you are looking for some guidance and understanding of personal protection insurance.

MANAGING DEBT

Overall, it is good policy not to get into debt. However, if it is an asset such as a house, where debt may be unavoidable, then the faster you can pay your debt off the better. When you are paying off your credit card every month during the interest-free period, this is paying off your debt. Where you are using a debit card instead of a credit card, this is also staying out of debt. When buying a house, the lower the debt the better. See if you can pay it off faster than is required. If you pay on a weekly basis then you will pay less interest long term, and even if you pay more than the necessary amount then the extra actually comes off the principal that you owe. Some of the more basic home-loan products have a lower interest rate, but no offset account. If you decide on a loan that has the capacity for an offset account, this can be useful in reducing the overall interest that you pay. If there is no offset account then you are probably paying a lower rate of interest. But make sure you check this.

With a home-loan account product it can be better to leave the interest rate on variable, particularly when rates are decreasing. Where rates are increasing, then you can think about fixing your interest rate for a few years at a time. However, fixed-term rates are usually a bit higher than current interest rates, to allow for increases over time. Variable rates are often lower, so you may view these as being preferable. However, if you want peace of mind and are not going to pay more off your mortgage than the institution requires, then fixing your rates for a few years may be appropriate. Make sure you discuss the options available to you with your institution's home loan manager.

BUDGETING

If you set yourself a budget and manage to work out what you need, you may be able to save some money for your future. Setting goals for your future will help you to achieve what it is you want. If you take a long-term view then you may find that you make better progress. Set one-year, five-year and ten-year goals. You may find that you can save money by doing things like cooking your own food instead of buying take-aways. This may also help you to eat better and be healthier. All the little bits add up. A big saving, if you are able to afford it and stretch the budget, is to purchase all your staples when they are on special. This means buying the cooking ingredients you use most often, such as flour, sugar, tea, coffee, butter/margarine, and tinned foods when they are at their cheapest, so that you have a replica store in the cupboard and you don't have to buy them at full price. This works well with cleaning and washing products too. You'll be amazed at the savings over a year. You might even be able to set aside enough for a nice holiday!

When you are shopping, whether for food, clothes or furniture, you can look for bargains. However, make sure that it's something that you need and are going to use. It's not a bargain if you don't need it, it's just a waste of money.

DEALING WITH DEBT

When you fall behind in paying off your loan, credit card, or utility bills, you may be contacted by a debt collector. If you disregard the debt collector and do not respond reasonably in relation to them, then they may sue you. This means that it will go to court and if you disregard this then it is likely that a judgement will be made against you.

It is better in the long run to initially contact the providers of the loan, credit card, or utility and enter into a payment plan with them. This stops the otherwise mounting debt from being passed on to a debt collector. Where your debt has already been passed on to a debt collector then the best thing to do is to enter into a payment plan with them. You should be honest about any other debts you have, and be realistic about your capacity to pay the debt back.

Be very wary of companies promising to help you get out of debt or consolidate it. They do not do this free gratis, and they may not even be able to do what they say they will. It is much better to access a financial counsellor connected to the government services. This service is free in Australia.

See the Money Smart website for more information on how to deal with debt collectors (4). Information is also on the Money Smart website on financial counselling, debt consolidation and refinancing, among other useful topics. There is a link discussing free legal advice, which is recommended at the point of contact from a debt collector, and also when there is a court proceeding against you.

It might be a good idea to arm yourself with some information about scams, so that you will be more likely to recognise one, and therefore avoid becoming a victim. Read about companies you should not deal with, such as companies that are unlicensed, the tricks used, and how to protect yourself, at the Money Smart scam page (5).

BANKRUPTCY IN AUSTRALIA

If you apply for voluntary bankruptcy you are allowed to nominate a registered trustee to attend to your case. Otherwise, the Official Trustee is appointed.

Consequences:
- Your income, employment and business may be affected. There may be restrictions placed on you.
- If you earn more than a certain amount you may be required to make compulsory payments to your Trustee.

- Most unsecured debts are covered by bankruptcy but there are some exceptions.
- Bankruptcy affects your ability to travel overseas.
- Your name will appear permanently on the National Personal Insolvency Index (NPII).
- It will affect your ability to obtain credit.
- Your Trustee may sell your assets.
- You may lose the right to take or continue legal action.
- Bankruptcy lasts for three years and one day, unless your Trustee objects, in which case it might be for a period of eight years.

To find out more information please go to (6).

BECOMING AWESOME

- Keep a journal of income and expenses, so that you can work out your average spending.
- Work out your needs and wants, and look at reducing the amount of the 'wants' column.

- See if you can save up for an emergency fund.
- Stay away from pay-day loans, if at all possible.
- Look to ethical microfinance companies if you need some money to pay for an emergency break down.
- Contribute to your superannuation, and have income protection insurance, as well as trauma cover, if you are employed.
- Increase your savings by choosing more economical options for socialising, reducing your clothing and lifestyle costs, buying food on special, and choosing to cook meals at home.
- Save up the deposit for your first home by remaining in the family home, if possible.
- By taking these steps, you can start having awesome financial responsibility.

Chapter 8

Work/Career

One of the ways we tend to define ourselves is by our work and career. Our self-esteem may be tied up in this and, in this case, if we are not working then our self-esteem takes a big hit. If you are not working, and it is not your choice, then you need to stay motivated to find work, or to find other ways to feel engaged with the world around you. Perhaps your situation means that at this time of life it isn't possible to work. In this case, engagement with others may be helpful to provide social support and meaning.

DECIDING WHAT TO DO

You may have made educational choices that follow your interests or your talents, and so you may have finished school with the best grades you can get in your best subjects. Whether you go on to university or go to TAFE and get an apprenticeship will depend on what you want to be and do. Nowadays, you cannot bank on having a job for life. It is expected that the generations coming through into the workforce over recent times will have a number of jobs and careers throughout their lives. When setting out on a career path, if you go towards something that already interests you, whether that is academic, being around animals or working with your hands, then you are more likely to find something you enjoy doing. In addition, you might be able to keep the number of changes of jobs down to a minimum. Changes may come where you try one area and find after a while that it doesn't work for you. Then you can carry it forward with you, see it as a learning experience and find something else. No learning is ever wasted.

In the case where you didn't do as well as you wanted at school, then all is not lost. It may be a good idea to have a gap year, and during this time investigate certain areas you are interested in. Perhaps gain some work experience and follow your interests.

You might consider going into a trade, where you learn on the job, along with some technical education. You might consider plumbing, electricals, or mechanics. In Australia, the technical courses you do are run by TAFE (Technical and Further Education) Colleges. Make an appointment with one of their course advisers for a run down on what the course entails, and have a discussion around making your choices.

Even if you did not get the best results for Year 12, you can still go to university if that is what you want to do. There is always mature-age entry, which is around twenty-five years of age. If you failed Year 12, you are able to do a qualifying year of study that means you can start your preferred course degree on completion. University is by no means the province of 19-20 year olds. Whether you pass Year 12 or not, you can go to university at any age. It can even be a better experience if you leave it until you are a little older, when you may be more certain that the degree you want to complete is the right one for you.

Where you don't want to do a trade or go to university then do your research around other training options. Explore the other TAFE courses and training available through various private institutions. There are many options and if you can settle on something you are interested in then you are on your way.

While your parents may be encouraging you to go into a particular career, you should really look at what that career involves and work out whether your personality traits and your talents are suited to that career. The question you can ask yourself is, 'Would I enjoy doing that?' It might be helpful to talk to a careers adviser and find out more about the tasks that are involved. Are those tasks activities that you can see yourself doing? Not all tasks in all jobs are necessarily fun. However, if you can see yourself being OK about doing them then that is one hurdle you will be able to jump. It is important to be able to see yourself enjoying the majority of the tasks, or at least to enjoy the result of engaging in those tasks. There must be an emotional payoff for you. Whether it is getting satisfaction from helping people, or creating something that you are proud of, you should be able to envisage or imagine positive outcomes.

ASSESSING YOURSELF

Think about careers that might use the talents you have and the subjects you are good at. Get careers advice. Talk to people. You can also do a careers interest survey, which was originally created by Holland (1). This is still valid and is available free online at (2). You can then look at the jobs that are involved in your interest profile. Holland splits up careers into six areas. They are: realistic, artistic, investigative, social, enterprising and conventional. Find your top three areas. Then you can think about which jobs you might like. This is only a first step, and you could investigate these possibilities further with a careers adviser or teacher. It also allows you to select and explore jobs in particular categories and at different education levels. If anything interests you, then you can take steps to find out more.

FUTURE PROSPECTS

There will probably be a revolution in the area of work with more artificial intelligence being utilised in the workplace. While this may mean that some jobs will disappear, other jobs will be created. In the short to medium-term future, however, it will be the jobs involving what we do best that will not be destroyed. Jobs involving communication and interpersonal skills are likely to be preserved, and even to increase in their importance (3). Consider these areas in your assessment of your work prospects and interests.

As we go through life our interests may change. We might become more interested in people and how the mind works, or there may be a growing interest in the economy or business. Sometimes it is difficult to really know what you want to do before you have had some life experience. There are some advantages to knowing what you want to do early on, but for many people who change careers having experience in a different field can also be of great benefit, as you will be bringing something outside the norm to your new career, which could give you an edge.

TRAINING

Aligning your interests and passions to the training you do will enable you to confirm that you have made the right career choice, or give you the opportunity to change direction if you feel that you have not made the right choice. There may be some aspects of training that you enjoy less than others, but if the majority of what you are doing and learning is interesting to you then stick with it. If, on the other hand, you find the subjects uninspiring or very difficult, then it might be a sign to rethink your goals. Review your interests and passions. Work out whether you are putting enough effort into your studies. In this way you can make an informed decision about your future.

WORK EXPERIENCE +

Trying out work positions before you take on a full-time job is a good experience. Work experience in some form can help you to sort out what you want to do, or at least what you don't want to do. Working at a café or fast-food outlet when you are young can stand you in good stead when older, as employers are always after experience. Summer jobs and work experience can be great for investigating options and finding out what you like and don't like. It's always helpful to be able to do a number of jobs, so that you have a fallback position if one doesn't work out.

It may be that you are looking for work, but have not yet been able to find anywhere to take you on. It is tough when you have the right qualifications, but you are just starting out and don't have the experience. Employers nowadays are less likely to be willing to train people. If you're finding it difficult to land a job, it is important not to give up. Try further afield, where this is practical.

TAKING UP OPPORTUNITIES

John's grandfather took him aside one day. He told him to always say, 'Yes' when someone asked him to do something. John asked, 'What if I can't do it?' His grandfather replied, 'You still say yes, and then you go out and learn how to do it.'

This means taking opportunities as they arise, as well as learning new ways of behaving and doing things. This opens up new pathways for you in life. It is worth noting that this is different to not being able to say 'No' if it is something you don't want to do or genuinely won't be able to do – you still need to set boundaries and be realistic.

EXPLORATION

When looking for work or changing employment, it is best to check advertisements as well as canvassing firms and businesses directly. There are some jobs that you may get through being headhunted or through your social networks. Explore traditional venues and websites. Make sure you have an updated curriculum vitae or resumé to send to prospective employers. It is also advantageous to have a cover letter for the specific job you are applying for. It is possible to find help from professional writers who specialise in CVs and resumés, and who know the best way to present them. As an alternative, there are some good books on writing CVs and resumés, which may give you the information you need to create a first-class CV of your own.

INTERVIEWS PLUS

In any interview, appearance and presentation is important. Dress as formally as the position warrants. It is better to be slightly overdressed than too casual. Good hygiene is necessary. It may be helpful to think about the questions you might be asked in an interview, and work out some good answers. You might know a business manager or someone who may do a mock interview with you. It is common to be nervous in a job interview. The more practice you can get the less nervous you will be and the better the outcome may be.

In exploring advertisements to apply for, sometimes it helps to be adventurous.

> Josh came across an advertisement for a copywriter. This was what he was interested in doing for a career. He was not sure that he had the experience and ability to get this job, but after thinking about it for a while he said to himself, 'What have I got to lose?' He applied for the position, and although he didn't have much experience, he gave thoughtful answers in his interview and was able to present a great portfolio of ideas he had created as examples of his work, even though they were only for imaginary companies. His engagement and initiative ended up landing him the job.

The moral of this story is to go for jobs that you might not get, even though you think it is not worth it. This holds for both men and women. You need to have confidence in your ability to work in a position that might be a little out of your comfort zone. All jobs are initially unknown, and it is perfectly normal to feel anxious and uncertain to start with. Just diving in might well be the right way to do it.

WORK RELATIONSHIPS

Where you are lucky enough to land a job, then you need to pay attention to your work relationships. Respect everyone, and treat them in the way you would like to be treated. If you prefer to keep some distance and just have minimum contact then this is your choice; you don't need to tell your co-workers your life story, but at least be friendly. Give yourself a couple of months to work out the culture and systems of communication that are in place. You can then choose how much you want to involve yourself with everyone at work. The culture of a workplace is more than the stated rules; it also includes the unspoken rules that exist in any group. Each company or business has a culture, and it may take a little while for you to figure it out.

Everyone may work hard during the week but go to the pub on Friday nights, for instance. You can decide whether you want to socialise with your workmates or not. In a general sense, where you are able to remain pleasant and assertive with your workmates, then you will maintain your independence. If you do become close friends with some people, then you may need to think about how this may impact on impartiality and neutrality, and what steps you can take to ensure you maintain your both your integrity and your friendships. You don't want to find yourself in a situation where you are asked to 'take sides', as this could cause problems either personally or professionally. While this may not be an issue it is something to consider, so that you can be prepared in the event that conflict does arise.

Work relationships can be easy or difficult, depending on personalities and status. If you are starting out at entry level, you may have a number of managers above you. At work, respect is the best value to show. This is not to say that you can't stand up for yourself. It is important to stand up for yourself if others are taking advantage of you too much. Knowing how to be assertive is helpful. You can set boundaries for yourself and others, and there is a right way of going about this. Assertiveness is not being aggressive, but it is looking after your needs and respecting the needs of others.

HOW TO SUCCEED IN THE WORKPLACE

Work is a serious business, so fooling around and practical jokes are probably a bad idea. However, that doesn't mean that you can't have a laugh about something, but it is better if this is not laughing at someone. Bullying and teasing are out of bounds. Respectful conversation and behaviour is called for. Being polite and helping when asked are behaviours that will be rewarded by more positive relationships.

If you want to have a good reputation amongst your colleagues then it is better to be on your best behaviour at all times, even at the Christmas party event or any team-building event.

Getting drunk, behaving stupidly or pairing off with a work colleague are not things that will help your reputation. Behave in ways that will show you are responsible, honest, reliable, and dependable. If you say you'll do something, then do it. If you maintain positive relationships with everyone possible then you will be in a stronger position if and when the time comes for you to step up to a more responsible role.

WHEN TROUBLE COMES

When an issue arises with a co-worker, whether a major disagreement or a minor disagreement, then it is better to sort it out with them straight away. It may be counterproductive to discuss the situation with other co-workers before you approach the person concerned. If you try to sort it out through being assertive, but after a couple of attempts it still doesn't get sorted, then you could approach your boss or manager. They should be able to help. If your manager is not responsive, you may wish to take things to a higher level. See the chapter on assertiveness for more information.

In a situation where you are being bullied by someone at work, then even if you are assertive it may be completely disregarded. It would be a good idea to analyse what is happening and talk to someone outside of work about it. Check to see if it qualifies as marginal bullying, which is generally just irritating; or qualifies as full-blown bullying, which makes you feel inadequate and helpless. If it is a co-worker bullying you then you can talk to your boss about it. If it's your boss, then your organisation should have a policy about workplace bullying and you could take your complaint to human resources or a specified person within the organisation. If you cannot get the help you require within your workplace, you may need to seek help from an official government body. There are national *anti-bullying laws* and state or territory health and safety bodies that can help people with *bullying* and harassment in the *workplace.* The Fair Work ombudsman should be the first point of contact to ensure your rights are being protected and upheld (4).

POSITIVE FEELINGS

Where everyone relates well with the others in a workplace then you will be more likely to feel good about going to work. If it is usually a happy place then feelings generated are more positive than when a conflict arises.

> Rachel has learnt to surround herself with people who make her happy. When she started out as a hairdresser she wasn't happy and was always being put down by the other hairdressers in the salon where she worked. She felt as though she was worthless and could never grow or become anything. When she lost her job at the salon she became so shut down that she didn't even want to be a hairdresser anymore, but after a while she found a new job at a salon where she was much happier. It took a while to find her confidence again, but it gradually happened. If she had known how different her experiences

of work life could be, she would have left her old job much sooner to become happier and be the best she could be.

It doesn't matter how many people you surround yourself with or how many friends you have, it's about surrounding yourself with those who make you feel it's worth waking up and going to work.

Another situation that is not uncommon in the workplace is sexual attraction. It could be helpful to consider the ramifications before you jump into a relationship. Issues to think about include workplace rules about such liaisons, and the possible consequences if the relationship doesn't work out. Would you feel comfortable continuing to work with, and possibly also socialise with, your former partner? Where your current employment is in an environment that you love and is providing you with great career opportunities, then explore what being in a relationship with someone who shares that environment with you could mean. Consider all aspects and talk about it with your prospective partner before diving in. It isn't that work relationships are not advisable, but rather that in some circumstances and in some organisations they are not conducive to promotion or positive outcomes in the long run.

SEXUAL HARASSMENT

Where you are being sexually harassed by your boss or someone who has greater power over you, then you may need to be quite careful. You may be able to tell the person that you want to keep the relationship on a professional level. However, if you feel intimidated and think that you might lose your job if you do this, then you may be able to think up something you could say that lets them let you know you're not interested, without them taking it personally, such as telling them you are already in a relationship. In any case, it would be a good idea to get support from a professional who may be able to help you think through the situation and deal with it in the best way possible.

BEING YOUR BEST

The best position to be in at work is to fit in but also maintain an element of independence. Doing a good job and upholding the rules of behaviour laid down by your workplace will mean that you are welcomed and valued as an employee. You can make up your own mind about what to share about yourself and what to keep to yourself. At least initially it is best to err on the side of caution and only share what you need to in order to carry out your job to the best of your ability. Essentially, your behaviour at work will actually give others some idea of who you are as a person. The more you can carry out your job in a pleasant and ordered way, the better the impression you will give. Thus, the better you will be thought of as an employee. Additionally, if you show respect to everyone you work with, are honest, and are able to be assertive, then you will be standing up for yourself and others, and feeling capable and empowered.

Once you are settled and happy in your place of work, you may have the opportunity to rise up the ranks. Such opportunities will depend on the organisation and the hierarchical structure of the positions within it. The higher you go, the more responsibilities you will have in relation to your work load, your employer, and any colleagues you are managing. This also holds true if you are in business for yourself and engage employees to work for you. Managing is an important role, and being a leader requires emotional intelligence and people skills. It is, however, a role that can be learned and practised, so there is hope if you are not a natural leader.

BECOMING AWESOME

- Choose a career that falls within your sphere of interests and skills.
- Ensure your talents and personality are in synch.
- Make sure work relationships are built around respect.

- Choose how little or how much you associate with people at work.
- Be assertive and stand up for yourself when you are being pressured to do too much.
- Seek help and support if you are being bullied.
- Carry out your work in a pleasant and efficient manner, and treat clients, employers and coworkers with respect, in order to be recognised as a valued employee.
- Take calculated risks to help to advance your career and ensure you continue to learn and grow.
- By taking these steps, you can begin to build an awesome career.

Chapter 9

Emotional Life

We are emotional beings. We use emotions throughout our day. We make value judgements using emotion, such as choosing one product over another, because we prefer the packaging or like the advert. A value judgement occurs when we decide that one thing is better than another. We feel emotions that are attached to events in our memories, and feel emotions as we experience situations throughout the day. The way in which making value judgements utilises the emotions is shown in those people who have brain injuries in the part of the brain that processes emotion. They find it impossible to choose one thing over another (1). Even in trivial choices we use emotion.

THE LOWDOWN ON EMOTION

When talking about emotion it is very helpful to use the right word, and to label the emotion. There are many words that describe emotions. A list that may not be comprehensive can be found at (2) and you are welcome to download it so that you can refer to it when you wish. By using the right word when talking to another person about how you feel, or what you felt, you will convey an accurate picture of what you are experiencing, or did experience. Communication then becomes better. The more accurate you can be with your descriptions of how you feel, the more others will understand you. If you say you feel bad, this does not convey a specific picture to another, whereas saying you feel guilty actually conveys a lot more to the listener and they will be able to understand your experience better.

In remembering events, we can easily recall the emotion we were feeling at the time. The more intense the emotion, the greater likelihood of us remembering the event. Once we are feeling a particular emotion then it seems as though there is a pathway in our brains that connects all the events that are attached to that particular emotion. So they are much easier to access.

We have discussed that emotions are attached to events or situations. Thoughts and feelings are also connected. Thoughts usually occur before the feelings or emotions are brought up to awareness. Sometimes we might think that the emotion just comes up, but it is likely in this case that the thought came up from our unconscious and did not stay in our awareness for long enough for us to realise it.

So if you consciously think more happy thoughts then your mood ought to change. This is likely to help in everyday situations, but may not work as well if you are particularly depressed. See the chapter on personal growth for further information on this issue.

In everyday situations, though, if you are motivated to do so, you may be able to change how you feel. It would help if you have a store of positive memories to call upon.

In recognising and labelling emotions we gain self-awareness in the present moment. The more we do this, the more we can increase our self-awareness. We can quite easily accept normal emotions. It's when we feel extremes of emotion, and particularly negative emotions, that we may need to take some action for ourselves. You can't make others do or feel what you want. You can only change yourself. People don't necessarily see things in the way you do. Everyone has different histories, values, beliefs, and ways of thinking. Emotions arise due to past experiences and thoughts, and your own set of experiences leads to the view you have of your world. It is possible to rise above this. You can do this by using empathy. That is, by putting yourself into someone else's shoes. Empathy is not sympathy. You are not going into your own emotions when you empathise. It is more about the understanding of where the other person is at. It is taking the bones of the other person's story and putting yourself in that story, and understanding how and why that person is feeling the way they are. You show empathy when you are able to actively listen to the other person and reflect back what they are feeling.

You may well be affected emotionally by the impact of others. There are things that you can do about this. Firstly, you can empathise with them. Sometimes just listening really helps. A situation can be discussed and sometimes, at a later date, options may be explored and solutions found and actioned. While it depends on what the situation is, your emotional reaction will be uniquely yours. This is due to your world view, past experiences, and the meaning that you place on whatever is happening.

SELF-MONITORING

As you go through your day you take note of what happens. Self-monitoring is taking a further step back from awareness, so that you are aware of being aware. You may like to flag particular situations so you can start self-monitoring when these situations arise. Take note of the sequence of events and behaviours, what you said and what they said, what you felt and what the end result was. This is the start. Now you have a baseline to work from and will be able to put new behaviours into place on the next occasion.

If you are in an unhealthy relationship, how do you recognise it? You may recognise that it is an unhealthy relationship when you realise that you feel more negative emotions when you are with the person, or when you are away from this person but thinking about them. If you feel sad because of what they do, if they say things that make you feel worthless, helpless, and hopeless, if they criticise you and put you down all the time, if they take advantage of you and you feel downtrodden, these are all signs that either the relationship itself needs to change or you need to get out of it. Where you approach your partner and ask for change but they refuse to engage in any relationship counselling or refuse to change their behaviour, then it may be time to seek individual counselling to change yourself and find support to remove yourself from that relationship.

HAPPINESS

Happiness is a state of mind, not an end result. People say that they will be happy when they achieve a certain thing or goal, whether it's a job, a partner, or something that is in the future. However, why wait to be happy when you can be happy as you go along towards these goals? You don't need to wait to be happy. All that needs to be happening for you is that you have some positive things to be grateful for. Then you can say to yourself, 'I am healthy, I am grateful for my health, I am grateful for my friends, I am grateful that I am progressing towards my goals.' Allow yourself to be happy for forward movement. Happiness is an uplifting of your spirit and positive feeling. It is also good for your immune system. Perhaps we are not going to feel happy every minute of the day, but you can feel happy most of the time. And then you can say that you are happy. Don't discount feelings of happiness just because you feel upset about something for a time. The positive feelings you have need to be taken into account. If you see yourself as making progress and you have a number of things to be grateful for, then you can feel positively about your situation and you can feel happy.

The more positive statements you can say to yourself about where you are at, the happier you will feel. Give yourself the benefit of the doubt and give yourself the chance to feel happy. You will find that everything looks better when you are feeling more positive, and then it is possible to spiral up rather than down. In the morning, or last thing at night, find at least three things that you are grateful for, and say them to yourself. Grateful people are usually happier people.

ANGER

All emotions are legitimate. Everyone feels anger at one time or another. The question is how you express your anger and whether you act in ways that have negative consequences for yourself and/or others. Just being shouted at can have negative consequences, let alone being the victim of violence. In nearly all circumstances violence is not the answer. In all day-to-day situations violence is unwarranted. The time when it is warranted is in self-defence against a physical attack. Otherwise, words are a better way to deal with a situation that makes you angry. Talking things through and using reasoning and logic is better. One strategy to manage your anger is to take yourself out of the situation for a time so that you can calm down. Then talk it through sensibly. Another is to count to ten before you reply. That might just be enough to take the edge off and allow you to reply when in a calmer state.

Becoming aggressive is not the answer to sorting out a situation. It will just make it worse. It is better to be assertive. In being assertive you state your needs in the situation and stand up for yourself. In addition, you take other's needs into account. Where you are assertive rather than aggressive or passive, then you are more likely to feel better about your behaviour, better about yourself, and better about the situation. When you address situations as they arise then you are less likely to explode with anger at a later date. You are able to state how you feel, and this allows some expression of your emotion, which in turn reduces the likelihood of bottling things up. See the chapter on assertiveness for more information.

Overall, statistics show that men are more violent towards women than the other way around (3). This may come down to societal values and norms. Just because this happens does not make it OK. Men need to change how they deal with anger and change how they think about women. Women are not property or objects. Men and women are equal partners in a relationship, and women need to be treated as such by all men.

DIFFICULT EMOTIONS

We will look at strategies to manage the more difficult emotions now.

Generally speaking, unless you consciously think about and dive into the more negative emotions, emotions will only last a certain amount of time. However, if you consciously go with them and think about all the times you felt that particular emotion, then you will feel that emotion for longer. If you don't feed it, you won't have it staying around. This is because your emotions are fed by your thoughts. If you think different thoughts then your emotions will change. There is a difference between dwelling on negative feelings and being aware of your emotions. By being aware, and focussing on what you are feeling, then the emotion may change by itself. This is the idea behind the book *Focussing* by Gendlin (4). Each time the emotion changes, you label it, and then keep on focussing on what you are feeling. Then it changes again.

Although different emotions are fed by our thoughts, we may have particular issues to which negative emotions are attached. In this case, we will continue to feel the negative emotions whenever we think about the event which triggers them, until the event or issue has been processed more completely and the emotion is detached from the event or issue. Processing the event or issue through counselling and psychotherapy is the best way to reduce the emotions attached to the event or issue. NLP and Time Line Therapy™ are also means of processing negative emotions.

So difficult emotions such as sadness and loneliness arise because we are thinking thoughts that bring these emotions up for us. They have meaning for us. Every emotion is normal and within the realm of human experience. All emotions are legitimate.

STRATEGIES TO MANAGE FEELINGS

There are different strategies to manage different emotions. Because people may feel the same emotion for different reasons, each person needs to find the action that works for them. If you feel sad, and if this is because you have experienced a loss of some kind, then it may be helpful to experience that sadness for a while, label it, explore the reason, and then focus on what you are doing. If you are feeling sad because of someone's actions or behaviour towards you, then acknowledge this to yourself, think about how you could act to redress this feeling, and work out what you can say in an assertive manner to the person responsible to try to change the situation. Sometimes action may be appropriate, and sometimes it isn't. Sometimes if you just focus on the feeling then the feeling may change to some other emotion, as discussed. So you need to give yourself time to feel it and you need to feel it in order to progress.

A strategy for managing the feeling of loneliness may be to take action to contact the outside world. This may be possible if you have someone to phone, whether a friend or a counselling service. The feeling of loneliness may go away after contact. Where you feel lonely but are in the midst of many people, then this may indicate the need for individual counselling to contact the inner you. Going out with friends, seeing family or phoning them, or even going out people-watching may be helpful strategies to reduce loneliness.

Envy and jealousy are emotions that are quite unnecessary. Sometimes it is more in our heads than an emotion.

What is the use of feeling that specific others have it better than you? You have your life and they have theirs. The strategy to dealing with these emotions is to consider yourself and your world as giving you the best at the current time. It is much better to be happy for others who have a good life, or who are in a better position than you. If you can be happy for them, then you are not condemning yourself to being in the same position forever. If you can be happy for others then you are giving yourself the opportunity to change to a better situation. Focussing on positive feelings is much better than focussing on negative feelings. What we focus on grows. Where you focus on lack, lack grows. Where you focus on abundance, abundance grows. So focus on positive things and emotions so that you will be able to notice opportunities to change your situation for the better.

FORGIVENESS

Another pointless action is that of revenge. If someone has hurt you it is much better to learn from the relationship and figure out how to do it better next time, rather than do something that will be essentially nasty and reprehensible. Think about what your actions would say about you as a person. Whatever you might do is not going to turn time back. They are much more likely to feel hard done by and resentful. And it is not going to change their general mode of operating and relating with others. So learn and move on. You cannot change their behaviour. You can only change yourself. The best thing you can do in this situation is to let go of your feelings towards them through forgiving them. This is not to say that you need to tell them. This forgiveness is an inner process that you do for yourself, so that the emotions don't fester inside you and harm you. You have the choice when you do this. It may not be the right time yet, if you have experienced deep trauma, for example. Self-forgiveness actually heals our unconscious mind and allows healing to take place at a deep level. This forgiveness exercise also seems to have a tangible effect on how you relate with others, as well as how you see yourself in relation to the person or people involved. You will feel freer and lighter.

> ## FORGIVENESS EXERCISE
>
> What you do is imagine the person standing in front of you, surrounded in pink light. Say out loud to them (it's probably best to do this alone), 'I ask your forgiveness, I forgive you, I forgive myself. I pray for your prospering wherever you are. I bless you and release you to your highest good'.
>
> This process will dissolve the emotions and allow you to move forward with your life. Do this also if you have guilty feelings about something you've done.

Resentment and frustration can be problematic feelings to overcome. Resentments usually build up over time. Sometimes they are prevalent within a primary relationship. Whenever an argument occurs, all the resentments come up and out to be raked over again. Again, you can try using the forgiveness exercise and see if the resentments dissolve. At other times, proper discussion and feeling heard is an important road to peace, for both parties. The same can be said about frustration. Something is not happening the way you want it to. Sometimes rational discussion and asking for behaviour change can be helpful. Relationship counselling may also be beneficial.

PROCESSING NEGATIVE EMOTIONS

Where you experience inappropriate amounts of negative emotions you may find Time Line Therapy™ helpful. While this process does not mean that you won't feel the negative emotion again, it is usual for the edge to be taken off, so that the excessive degree of the emotion dissolves. Time Line Therapy™ can be provided by an NLP Practitioner who has trained in the Tad James tradition. This therapy could be pursued alone or in conjunction with other NLP therapy or, depending on the practitioner, when working on your issues with the aim of self-change.

Meditation and mindfulness can be useful in reducing the amount of reactivity you feel on a daily basis. Counselling, including psychological counselling and psychotherapy are also useful. If you can find someone to teach you the Emotional Freedom Technique (EFT) then you can practice this yourself, which would help you to become more in control of your emotions.

WHEN UNDERSTANDING OTHERS' EMOTIONS IS DIFFICULT

If you can't understand the emotional lives of other people or have an inability to understand how or why they feel particular ways, then you may lack empathy. If you think you have this feature, or know someone who has, then there is something you can do about it. Should you believe you lack empathy, then the idea is to try to understand what it is like for others to experience emotions. Even if you understand on a mental level, this is helpful. It may be impossible for you to understand on an emotional level. The object is not to exploit this understanding, but to be able to know what others are feeling at times when it might be important for you to show some understanding. Showing empathy makes relationships stronger. If you are able to show care and concern for others you will find your relationships improve.

If you know someone who appears to lack empathy, or admits to it, then you can also do something that may help. You can explain the cause and effect equations of the emotions you are feeling. Hopefully, this will help the other person to at least mentally understand what is happening for you. Another thing you can do is just accept that they will never really get you and your feelings. There may always be a gap there. You could also consider how exploited you may feel, and think about how much this matters to you. You may choose to act, or otherwise. The choice is yours. In as much as all circumstances are uniquely individual, counselling may be helpful for anyone who is struggling with issues around empathy.

BECOMING AWESOME

- Understand that all emotions are legitimate and that we operate on emotion on a day-to-day basis.
- Learn to recognise that thoughts and emotions are linked.
- Work towards living in the present moment more and being grateful for what and who you have in your life, in order to increase more positive emotions of happiness, joy and love.
- Explore the different ways that negative emotions can be processed, away from the events in your mind.
- Consider mindfulness or counselling, if you are feeling overwhelmed by negative thoughts and emotions.
- Allow yourself to feel your emotions, and know and understand that this is part of the process of letting go.
- If you can accept your emotions, and not allow them to control your

behaviour in negative ways, then you are becoming awesome.

Chapter 10

Mental Health

What is mental health? It is easier to describe mental health as the absence of mental-illness issues, rather than utilising more positive words.

However, when you are mentally healthy you have a clear mind, you are able to focus on what you are doing, you are acting in the world without fear, and making progress towards your goals. There is nothing specifically that is bothering you, you communicate reasonably well and feel that you are an agent of change in your life. Although you may not be perfect and could possibly make some changes, you are essentially an effective human being. Your emotions are generally neutral to positive, and you are usually able to let negative thoughts go.

When mental-health issues arise these above aspects may change, and your way of being in the world differs. Examples of this include:

- you usually have a clear mind and it starts to get less clear
- you are no longer able to focus on what you used to focus on because of competing thoughts and emotions
- you find you are fearful of something specific happening to you or loved ones
- you suddenly change your goals to something others would not agree with
- you find specific issues or things start to bother you a lot and interfere with your daily life
- your emotional life changes to very negative or very positive but destructive
- you now dwell on very negative thoughts and are unable to think positively

While these are some things to watch out for, even if it does happen, you are not alone. It's helpful to get a professional opinion and to seek appropriate treatment where applicable. About 45% of people experience mental illness in the course of their lifetime, so it is very common. You are, therefore, not abnormal should you encounter such a challenge.

DEPRESSION

We have discussed how thoughts and feelings/emotions are connected and how it is possible to change your mood. Sometimes, the emotion is so powerful that trying to change it consciously is just too difficult. In this case, your brain chemicals may be having a powerful effect, so it may take longer to effect some change in the way you are feeling. As previously discussed, a particular emotion allows access to memories of similar states, and the thoughts that go with them. These feelings and thoughts can override conscious efforts to think of more positive things. However, it is still worth making the attempt. Thinking of possible positive outcomes and benefits may help. There may be a positive in the situation that you are unable to see at the time. Talking with someone may be helpful in this situation. You can try your family and friends for a start. Where you are still feeling down, then find a counsellor or psychologist. Having counselling from a trained professional has been shown to be helpful in recovery from depression (1). It may take some weeks, but you can change your thinking around your situation. Exercise is also helpful for depression, as is engaging in activities that usually make you happy. You might be depressed due to an event in your life or because your life is not going in the way you really want. A counsellor can be a good sounding board, and can help you set some realistic and specific goals that you can take action towards. You may then see the light at the end of the tunnel.

Where you are clinically depressed, which is further down the road to feeling hopeless or helpless, then your GP can refer you to a psychologist with a mental-health care plan (in Australia). Sometimes medication may be indicated, but make sure that you discuss the possible side effects with your doctor or psychiatrist, if you are referred to one. Make an informed decision whether to go on medication or not. Ensure that your doctor makes up a health-care plan of six-twelve sessions and refers you to a psychologist. It may be that you are able to recover with some lifestyle changes, such as diet, exercise and seeing the psychologist. A study recently completed found that the Mediterranean diet improved the mood of people suffering depression (2). Medication is really just a temporary solution, and what you need is a long-term solution.

> May's father died the day before her daughter was born. May was twenty-four years old. Initially, no-one told her about his death. She was in hospital and he was in the mortuary. Eventually she found out. She went into a deep depression, as she had been very close to her father. People ignored her and didn't know what to do. Her doctor tried to send her to a psychiatrist. She went, but walked out of the consultation, as it didn't feel right. She was suffering a combination of post-natal depression and depression related to grief. It took her seven years to get over it by herself.

The reasons for depression can be complex, and so taking control of your own treatment and approach, and finding the best counsellor or psychologist for you is a very important aspect of recovery.

GRIEF AND LOSS

As we go through life there are times when we are going to feel down. Events may occur that have a negative impact on us. Whether you are unemployed and can't find work, you lose your job, have a relationship break up, lose a friend, or experience the death of a loved one or friend, it is very normal to feel depressed and sad for a while. It is quite OK to feel sad, down, and unhappy, but is important to go through the grieving process and work through your emotions and thoughts about your loss so that you can eventually feel more positive about life. When a loss is experienced, the more dear and close the person or thing, the more impact it will have on you (3). Everyone grieves in their own way, and there are large differences between people. You might find that you are expressive and find yourself crying a lot. Or you just might feel a profound sadness. Both of these responses, and all the possible behaviours in between, are fine. At the beginning you will be in shock and probably feel numb for a while, and initially you may disbelieve the news. Numbness may last up to a week or two, but eventually the reality of the situation is accepted, at least on a mental level. After the shock of the loss has worn off, a large range of emotions and thoughts may arise for you. Anger, sadness, grief, and loneliness are common. During the next six weeks or so emotions come up and symptoms may occur, such as difficulty sleeping, loss of concentration, thoughts of the person you have lost, and many others. The reality of the loss also needs to be accepted on an emotional level during this time (3).

Worden (3) suggests that there are four tasks that people need to traverse when experiencing a loss. The first task is to accept the reality of the loss. This occurs on two levels; firstly, mentally;

and secondly, emotionally. The second task is to process the pain of loss. The third is to adjust to a world in which the deceased is missing. The fourth is to find a continuing bond with the deceased while embarking on a new life. While these tasks are specifically for people experiencing the loss of a loved one, the tasks are actually equally true for any other type of loss. For instance, if you lost your job then you would need to accept the reality of that loss, to experience the pain of that loss, to adjust to a world in which you no longer have that job and then to move on, despite the fact that you lost your job so that you may find another job or otherwise embark on a new life and find new beginnings.

ANXIETY

Everyone experiences anxiety, but some people experience it more than others, and the anxiety becomes debilitating. We all have anxiety over how we'll go in tests at school, in exams at Year 12, and when we need to perform well, such as in job interviews. Some people experience anxiety in social situations, while others have a fear of public speaking. Every individual is different. When the anxiety is more of a fear of a particular object or animal, then it is classed as a phobia. People may have a phobia about animals, such as spiders or snakes, and situations, such as height. Phobias are irrational fears. Anxiety is also a fear, but it's not as concentrated as a phobia. If we are anxious we worry about an issue or event. Often our worries don't eventuate. However, that doesn't mean that it is necessarily easy to stop worrying.

In our current world of connectedness and technology there are new fears and anxieties emerging. One in particular is the fear of missing out or FOMO. This is the fear that you are being or may be excluded from where it's all happening among your online friends. This means that people check their phones continually and can't bear being disconnected for long. An Australian Psychological Society survey carried out in 2015 (4) found that one in ten Australians reported that keeping

up with social-media networks was a source of stress for them. It also found that social media can reduce stress, with about 57% of Australians reporting this effect. Social media dominates the lives of Australian teens. More than half of all teens find it difficult to relax or sleep after spending time on social media, and 60% feel brain burnout from constant connectivity. Half of all teens experience FOMO, while a quarter of adults experience FOMO. You would be at risk for FOMO if you believe the following:
- it is important that friends' in-jokes are understood
- your friends are having more rewarding experiences than you
- it isn't OK for your friends to have fun without you
- missing out on planned get togethers is something to worry about (4)

If you are one of those who are always connected and get anxious over the issues listed here, then it might be a good idea to wean yourself off social media. The friends that ought to matter more to you are those that you meet in the flesh. With these friends, you can use your phone to contact them by ringing them. Meeting in person and talking about topics of interest to you is what progresses relationships. Reduce your social media presence. Talk to your friends on the phone or in person. That is of much more value in the greater scheme of things.

Wean yourself off social media so that you give it a good break during the day. At work, only check during breaks – the rest of the time you should be working. Outside of work see if you can get checking down to no more than once per hour. You could start by making the gaps between checking progressively longer, moving from ten minutes to twenty minutes and so on, up to one hour. This may be somewhat difficult, but persist! You may find that distracting yourself works best. Electromagnetic waves actually are stimulating to your brain, and this is one reason that sleeping becomes difficult, so ensure you stop engaging with social media or checking your phone for at least an hour before you go to bed.

ANXIETY DISORDERS

It is possible to be anxious about any number of things. Anxiety is fear of the future and what might happen. On one level it can come out in worry. If it becomes strong and has a negative impact on your life then it might be a good idea to get some treatment for yourself.

PANIC ATTACKS

If you have a panic attack, you may experience the following symptoms:
- you feel that you are having a heart attack
- you think you are going to die
- you have an urge to go to the toilet
- you need to get out of the situation you are in as fast as possible

The best way to manage a panic attack is to breathe slowly, or even to hold your breath for a little while. If your breathing speeds up, as commonly happens when you are anxious, then you hyperventilate and feel even worse. So breathe slowly, tell yourself you are not going to die, you are not having a heart attack, you are going to be fine and that you can get through this time. The most effective way of managing panic attacks is to find a professional who uses behavioural therapy in conjunction with exposure therapy. This means that you actually attempt increasingly difficult situations and, after you have completed the first one successfully, then you go to the next difficult one. This also includes some cognitive behavioural therapy in disputing the beliefs and thoughts that you have when in the difficult situations.

GENERALISED ANXIETY DISORDER

There is a disorder called Generalised Anxiety Disorder where people who have it are anxious about more than one thing usually, and specific things mostly. There is no focus for the anxiety, except the future and what it might hold for oneself and for others. This must be a difficult situation to be in, especially when life is a series of present moments and the future is not that far away. To live perpetually in dread and fear is very harmful to the body since the fight/flight response is triggered continually, and so the body becomes stressed. This can then cause further illness through the immune system being compromised. There is also an intolerance for uncertainty and a need for reassurance from others.

A number of treatments may be useful for someone with this disorder. Cognitive Behavioural Therapy delivered by a psychologist could work. Other processes that may work are mindfulness, meditation, and hypnosis. The person needs to relearn how to think about events in life, and to find more adaptive strategies to approaching the future. If you have Generalised Anxiety Disorder, then finding the right treatment for you will help you become less anxious.

EATING DISORDERS

Eating disorders indicate issues around control. Two common eating disorders are Anorexia Nervosa and Bulimia Nervosa (5). In Anorexia, the sufferer puts strict controls on how much food and sometimes water they take in. There is a particularly high risk of fatality with this disease. In Bulimia, there is a pattern of gorging and purging so that the sufferer loses the nutrition that would otherwise be provided by the food eaten. Both of these conditions may affect both sexes and any age. However, they appear to be most common among young people. Anxiety about body image often affects girls and boys, where social media and advertising communicate what society sees as the ideal body. Concern about eating can start off slowly but end up as anorexia or bulimia.

With Anorexia Nervosa, the individual may take in such a small amount of food that long-term health effects occur. Provided the sufferer does not starve him or herself to death, but gets appropriate treatment, then these negative effects may be lessened. The sufferer may not just starve him or herself, but may engage in huge amounts of exercise as well. This is all in the name of becoming the ideal weight. One aspect of the disease is that sufferers have a very distorted view of themselves and see themselves as fat when they are emaciated.

With bulimia, there is a pattern of binge eating followed by purging – whether by forcing oneself to vomit, or through use of laxatives. This means that very little of the food is absorbed by the body. The vomiting may be seen as a self-punishment for eating. For a recovery story from bulimia see (6).

Since societal norms of the ideal body have some input into sufferers' experiences, the more such ideas are discussed in the home, the better. It is a fact that young boys and girls who have not yet reached puberty are not yet at their adult body shape, and even then that body shape is fluid until the late teens and early twenties. Discussion around such concepts may be helpful.

Treatment requires ongoing support and belief-changing therapy through an Eating Disorders program. Another option would be cognitive behavioural therapy with an experienced psychologist. Alternatively, you could try NLP. In this way you can target the beliefs directly and change them. The important thing would be to have such treatment under the supervision of a doctor.

AVOIDANT RESTRICTIVE FOOD INTAKE DISORDER (ARFID)

ARFID is another eating disorder (7). It is similar to Anorexia in relation to the limitations in the amount or type of food consumed, but unlike Anorexia it doesn't involve any distress about body size or fears of being fat. There may, however, be fear of choking or fear of eating new foods. There are highly selective eating habits, which may be based on the colours or textures of food. While children may go through phases of picky eating, a person with ARFID doesn't consume enough food to grow and develop normally, so that stalled weight and growth may occur. In adults, not enough food is consumed to maintain basic body function. Supplements could be the only way to enable nutrition to be maintained.

Problems may arise at school and work due to psychosocial issues, including concerns about eating with others (7).

The best thing to do is to get treatment from a trained professional. Treatment does help to alleviate the issues.

BINGE EATING DISORDER

Binge eating disorder is a bit similar to Bulimia, without the purging behaviour. Often, food is binged on even when the person isn't hungry. Food may be eaten to forget thoughts and feelings. However, feelings of depression, guilt and disgust may arise after the binging behaviour. The person may engage in sporadic fasts and repetitive diets in response to the negative feelings evoked. Binging is often done secretly and alone. Approximately 47% of people with an eating disorder suffer from binge eating disorder (8). Low self-esteem is common, as is a negative body image. If you think this is what you have then seeking treatment is your best option.

A psychologist, counsellor or NLP practitioner may be helpful.

ORTHOREXIA NERVOSA

This is a disorder that may develop from healthy eating patterns (8). If you are a healthy diet enthusiast and develop anxiety around eating healthily then this may turn into a problem. A problem might be beginning if you find that: your healthy eating is taking up a lot of your time and is interfering with your daily life; if eating any food you regard as unhealthy leaves you feeling anxious and impure; if your sense of peace and sense of self is based on the purity and rightness of the food you eat; if you have gradually decreased the number of foods you feel are healthy for you; or if your health has actually deteriorated in recent times (9).

If you have become obsessed with healthy eating and will go to great lengths to ensure that you are eating healthily and can say yes to any of the above then think about taking some action to reduce your obsession. While it is good to have a balanced diet and to eat more healthy food than not, there is a point at which it becomes too much. It is important to remain balanced, rather than go to the extremes. However, where you allow yourself the occasional unhealthy food and cannot identify an obsession with healthy eating then you are likely to be just fine. Otherwise, find a professional who can help you.

PHOBIAS

People can also develop phobias. A phobia is an irrational fear of a specific object, whether animal or thing. Usually, there is a starting event for when the object became a thing of high anxiety and fear. There is an irrational fear that is evoked whenever the object is perceived. Such examples may be spiders, snakes, lizards, dogs, fear of heights, fear of public speaking and so on. These are simple phobias, which usually develop in childhood. In treatment, a good approach is Cognitive Behavioural Therapy using graduated exposure treatment. Alternatively, another treatment for simple phobias is

NLP. This stands for Neuro-Linguistic Programming and it is a system including techniques and processes that help to align the conscious mind with the unconscious mind.

There are also a wide number of more complex phobias, including social phobia and agoraphobia (fear of open spaces).

SOCIAL PHOBIA

People can develop social phobia where they get anxious in social situations. While many of us may get anxious in social situations when we meet new people, it becomes debilitating when your anxiety goes way up and you find you need to get out of the situation. Meeting new people is not the only situation that those suffering social anxiety find difficult. There is also the situation in using public transport. Meeting peoples' eyes would be problematic as well. So it can be very limiting of one's lifestyle where any social outing is a problem. St Vincent's hospital in Sydney has a good program for social phobia, and the program is also available as an online program that you do by yourself (10). It involves putting yourself in gradually more difficult situations and becoming acclimatised to them. In this way, you become comfortable with each level as you go up in the order of difficulty. In reality, it is exposure therapy. Hypnosis with imaginal rehearsal could also be helpful.

AGORAPHOBIA

Agoraphobia is a fear of open spaces, and often those who have it can't go very far from their home. Being housebound can be particularly debilitating to one's life and what one can achieve. Again, NLP can be helpful, as can a combination of cognitive behavioural therapy and hypnosis, as well as behavioural therapy and exposure therapy. Finding a good therapist who will visit the home is crucial, as is addressing all the psychological aspects related to the condition.

If someone you know experiences anxiety or a phobia of some kind, it isn't helpful to tell them to just get over it. The anxiety is an automatic response that is hardwired in the brain. There are ways of loosening the connections, but it usually takes time and specific techniques.

POST-TRAUMATIC STRESS DISORDER

Post-Traumatic Stress Disorder may come about when a person suffers an extraordinary loss, witnesses or experiences a traumatic event, has been in a life-threatening situation, or experiences a man-made or natural disaster. Symptoms may include re-experiencing the traumatic event in dreams or flashbacks, hypervigilance, avoidance of anything connected with the trauma, being easily startled, and numbness. It helps to talk about the trauma, and prolonged exposure also helps (imagining it in their mind) (9).

Psychological counselling with a specialist in trauma may be appropriate. There is also an online course available through St Vincent's Hospital, Sydney (10). Alternatively, Cognitive Behavioural

Therapy is appropriate and, in addition, there is EMDR (Eye Movement and Desensitisation Reprocessing), which can be administered by a psychologist who has had the correct training. Both these last treatments are evidence-based.

OBSESSIVE COMPULSIVE DISORDER

In obsessive compulsive disorder the obsession is the thought or image that recurs, and the compulsion is the ritual or act that is performed to neutralise the thought. Checking and cleaning are common (11). Often, the checking or cleaning needs to be absolutely perfect before the thought is negated, so a lot of time can be taken up in these rituals and the impact on daily living can be enormous. Treatment may involve exposure and response prevention, which is behaviour therapy, or some people may respond to cognitive behavioural therapy. There are some specific treatment centres available, so explore in your area for these services (10).

PSYCHOSES

To have a psychotic breakdown, two situations usually happen. Firstly, there is a genetic component; and secondly, the environment triggers or turns on the gene. This means that factors such as stress, age, or what is ingested or inhaled, can spark off an episode of psychosis. A number of drugs can also cause psychosis (12).

The main psychoses are bipolar disorder and schizophrenia.

BIPOLAR DISORDER

Bipolar is a mood disorder in which a person cycles between mania – feeling euphoric, and depression – feeling very down. In mania, the thoughts are fast, and fantasy may play a large role so that the person can get themselves in all sorts of trouble. The depression can be so low that the person can become dangerously suicidal. The cycling through these two states can be quick or slow, with a number of months in each state. One of the drugs used to treat bipolar disorder is lithium, which, if first taken when in a manic state, helps the person to balance out. Some people go off the medication because they don't like not feeling the way they feel when in the manic state. As a result, medication compliance can be an issue. However, in order to have a balanced and trouble-free life medication is recommended. Medication is something that may relieve most of the symptoms of psychosis, but is not a cure for it. Taking medication for the rest of your life is the best option. It is always a good idea to find out the possible side effects of the drug being suggested. The fewer side effects, the better. However, each individual has their own unique body chemistry, so different drugs may affect different people in unique ways. That is why it may take some time to find the right drug that works for you.

Psychotic illnesses often start in the late teens and early twenties when stress may be experienced in one's life. It can also start later in life. If your family has some members who have had a psychotic illness then you have a greater chance of being affected yourself. Even so, it is not a huge risk, and don't forget that environmental circumstances need to kick off the gene expression that you may or may not have.

SCHIZOPHRENIA

The other major psychotic illness is schizophrenia. This is a thought disorder, and when in the throes of an episode there is often delusional thinking and visual hallucinations. Usually, there are voices in one's head that are experienced as real and outside of the self. What will be experienced, as in the story that is lived, is very individual. There is schizophrenia and paranoid schizophrenia. In the paranoid version there are often delusions of persecution in some way. If there are no persecution beliefs, then a diagnosis of schizophrenia may be given. In this event there may be delusional beliefs of being a world saviour or something similar. There may be religious overtones or there may not. In any case, the delusions tend to be consistent with the world-view and personality of the sufferer, so they are very unique. Since the delusions and hallucinations are experienced as reality, the person's behaviour may be bizarre to the outsider. If, for instance, you believe that animals are saying nasty things to you then you may try to avoid them. If you believe that there are cameras everywhere and that you are on the internet (when this is not the case in reality) then it is likely that you will behave in a way that is congruent with this belief. So it can be extremely frightening, for the person suffering the delusions and for those around them.

Contrary to popular belief, schizophrenia is not a split personality. Rather, it is a thought disorder that adheres strongly to the conscious and unconscious mind of the sufferer.

Since bizarre behaviour gets noticed by families, and sometimes by the authorities, such behaviour may lead to treatment. There are some better drugs around now, which are more beneficial in symptom relief. Again, it might be necessary to try medications until you find the right one or the right combination. Should you come off the medication some time after the first episode and have another psychotic episode then that is a sign that you may need to be on medication for the rest of your life.

It is a good idea to be under a good psychiatrist for a reasonable time, because they are experienced in treating mental illness and psychoses. A normal GP is not qualified to treat these things, so ensure that you get a referral to a psychiatrist. GPs may be reliable in prescribing antidepressants for depression, but it would be safer to get a referral to see a psychiatrist in the first instance.

There is some evidence that marijuana triggers schizophrenia in some people (12). The inhalation of this drug would therefore be seen as an environmental factor that triggers the condition in those who are susceptible. Thus, should schizophrenia be in your family history then it might be an idea to stay away from marijuana.

STIGMA

Mental illness may be temporary or it may be lasting. There is perhaps more public recognition and acceptance of it now than there used to be. Well-known people have come out with their mental illness and struggles, so there may not be quite as much stigma associated with it now, but there is still some.

MANAGING A MENTAL ILLNESS

It is important to find a way to manage your mental illness. It is probably healthier not to let your mental illness define who you are. You are a person who has values, needs, and desires, who just happens to also have a mental illness. You are not your mental illness. You are more than your mental illness. While talking about your troubles, breakdowns and so on may be beneficial sometimes, if you talk about these things at every opportunity then you are letting your illness define who you are. You are more than your latest episode. Talk about things such as your goals and hobbies, what you'd like to do, and your dreams.

Wherever you are at, it is important to keep yourself safe. Recognise the triggers for your issue and find a professional who can help you manage your mental health. Ensure you ask medical professionals about the side effects of any medicine. The fewer the side effects you suffer, the better. There are now some better medications on the market.

Where you have been told that you need to be on the medication for the rest of your life, it is wise to heed this advice. Just because you feel better when on the medication doesn't indicate that the problem is fixed. It is just that the symptoms are under control with the medication.

No matter what the mental-health issue is, it is important to find support. A psychiatrist could be the first support, and it would be important to also find a psychologist or counsellor to talk with. They could help you manage your emotions, and discussion around thoughts and feelings may be very beneficial for you. In addition, they will be able to help you decide on the best coping mechanisms that will stand you in good stead through this time. Discussion about your life in general, and working out your goals and how to achieve, them may turn your life around, particularly if you are feeling depressed.

It is helpful to find activities that you enjoy and to engage in them. This will enable you to forget about your situation for a time, or at least help you to manage it better. One thing that may help is being in nature. Whether this entails going for a walk, or being in a garden, surrounding yourself with plants and living things can be very healing. There has been greater recognition of the healing aspect of gardens in recent times for both physical and mental issues. Being in nature is grounding and lifts the spirits. So get out in the garden and do some gardening for a while, or go for a walk where there are some trees, and you will find that it soothes and relaxes you.

RECOVERING FROM A MENTAL ILLNESS

The best reason for being on medication is to alleviate symptoms while you are engaging in treatment that has been shown to be helpful in the long term: such as behaviour therapy for phobias and anxiety; cognitive behaviour therapy for depression and OCD; and specific programs for eating disorders and OCD. Once treatment has been completed, then the medication may be reduced and stopped under the supervision of your doctor.

If you have had your mental-health issue for a long time, then recovering may present some difficulties. Since you will be used to behaving in certain ways, and thinking certain thoughts, there is likely to be a time of transition to being free to behave in different ways. It may feel strange, and weird, or it might be unsettling. Replace the nervousness that you may feel, and label it excitement. Then you may manage this time better. Be excited about what you might discover about where you are now. Notice what is different and be happy with the positive changes. Go with the flow. This is the new you. Take a few low-level risks, such as socialising with friends in a safe situation without drugs or alcohol, and see how that feels. Behave as you would like to behave, taking into account how you were before this issue came up for you. If there's anything you want to change, now is the ideal time to start putting those changes into place.

With mental-health issues, the thing that gets knocked around most is your self-esteem. So take time to be kind to yourself, surround yourself with positive people and build up your self-esteem. Work on building a skill, getting better at some activity, or building relationships. You can do these things whether or not you have recovered from your illness. This is also part of the management process. Engaging in counselling should also be beneficial.

RECOGNISING MENTAL ILLNESS

How do you recognise mental illness in yourself or in someone else?

This list is not exhaustive, but there are a few things to watch out for:
- Withdrawing from social interaction, isolating yourself
- Thoughts of self-harm, feeling hopeless, helpless and depressed
- Engaging in unusual behaviours
- Have moments of staring off into space
- Concern about persecution
- Preoccupation with food
- Concern about being fat, when not
- Fears/behaviours interfering with living
- Talking fast, doing everything fast, getting into trouble spending
- Getting into trouble with the police, when not usually criminal
- Talking about god, the devil, demons, etc.

BECOMING AWESOME

- Be aware that everyone experiences times of feeling down or depressed in their lives.
- Consider finding yourself some treatment if you are very down or clinically depressed.
- Seek counselling if you are having difficulties with experiencing the loss of someone or something, in order to help you through the grieving process.
- Get treatment for anxiety if it's adversely affecting your life.
- Don't be afraid to ask for help.
- Take time to find the right person to help you.
- Wean yourself off social media, or get help, if you feel you have FOMO.
- Consider NLP as a treatment for phobias.
- Acknowledge that you are more than your illness, you are more than your thoughts and behaviour. You are a unique human being and should accept that you are still awesome. If you suspect you are

bipolar or schizophrenia or if you are diagnosed with these conditions then get treatment.
- Find the right program or the right psychologist to treat eating disorders. Don't delay. It's important to get treatment due to the rate of fatalities, especially with Anorexia Nervosa. By getting the right treatment you will find that you end up with a much better quality of life than you would otherwise have.
- Remember: you are not alone.
- By taking these steps can become awesome at managing your mental health.

Chapter 11

Addictions

Addictions may involve physical dependence on a substance, and/or a psychological dependence. In the brain, the reward system is triggered when we behave in a certain way, for instance ingesting a particular substance, and we can become addicted to chasing this initial feeling, Some substances are actually very addictive and rapid in their effect, while others are somewhat less addictive. Sometimes one person may become addicted, while another may not. It is a very individual response since we all have unique brain chemistry and unique ways of thinking about things such as attitudes and beliefs, that may influence our behaviour when it comes to addictions.

If you find you are addicted to something you can take steps to rehabilitate yourself. Whether you manage this by yourself or with help will depend upon your specific addiction and your past history in relation to it.

COMMON ADDICTIONS

The substances that people most commonly become addicted to and dependent on that causes major problems are alcohol, nicotine, and drugs. Each substance can be difficult to withdraw from, and it takes a great amount of determination and effort. However, it is possible, and all is not lost if you are addicted. There is hope. As with any addiction or dependence, the more times that you try to give up, the more likely you are to succeed. It's about finding the strategies that are going to work for you.

There has been some discussion over the years as to whether there is such a thing as an addictive personality. Someone with an addictive personality has a higher likelihood of developing an addiction. There may be something in this, but it is by no means set in stone. While those people who tend to be dependent on others may be more susceptible to becoming dependent on substances, there is more evidence suggesting that availability and peer pressure are likely to help a person to get started on a particular substance.

With most addictive substances, and particularly drugs, there is a high when you initially take it. People may become addicted from this first rush. However, the body quickly becomes used to the drug, and so a greater quantity is required to feel the high, and even to feel normal. As a result, there is a continual searching to recapture the feeling that came from the first high.

ALCOHOL

In 2013 6.5% of Australians drank daily. 37.8% drank weekly (over 14 years old). Alcohol is the most widely used drug (1).

Alcohol can have toxic effects on your body. It is classified as a group 1 carcinogen, which means it causes cancer. Cancers particularly related to alcohol are those of the mouth, throat, tongue and liver.

Excessive alcohol consumption is a cause of a wide range of health and other harms, including being the major cause of road and other accidents,

> domestic and public violence, crime, liver disease, and brain damage, as well as contributing to family breakdown and broader social dysfunction.
>
> Lifetime risky drinkers are those who consume more than two standard drinks per day. Single occasion risky drinkers are those who consume four or more standard drinks on one occasion.

The more you drink, and the more often you drink, the higher is your risk for alcohol-related diseases.

Alcohol is a nervous system depressant. It has been associated with a range of diseases that may cause death and adverse effects that reduce the quality of life. These include: cardiovascular disease, cancers, diabetes, nutrition-related disorders, excess weight and obesity, risks to unborn babies, liver diseases, mental-health conditions such as depression and anxiety, dependency, long-term cognitive impairment, and self-harm.

TWELVE CONDITIONS LINKED TO CHRONIC HEAVY DRINKING

- Anaemia
- Cancer
- Cardiovascular disease
- Cirrhosis
- Dementia
- Depression
- Seizures
- Gout
- High blood pressure
- Infectious diseases – due to immune system being suppressed
- Nerve damage
- Pancreatitis

(2)

There is now some evidence that alcohol has serious adverse effects on growing brains. Since the brain is still growing up to the age of twenty-five then ideally you should limit your alcohol use until after this age. Of course, even after this age, copious amounts of alcohol are still going to damage your brain and your health (1).

Both binge drinking and daily drinking are problematic. However, because drinking in Australia seems to be such a large part of our culture, there may be an issue for you in the situation where you stop drinking but still socialise with your friends. There is more recognition now about the effects of alcohol, and people may well be more tolerant of others not drinking. If you decide to go down this path then while it may test some of your friendships, it may be very good for your health.

In the situation where you decide to limit your drinking, but not to stop completely, then you can limit your intake to no more than four standard drinks on one occasion. And if you are drinking daily, then limit your consumption to one to two standard drinks with a break of two to four days per week. When it comes to drinking and driving, society is now more accepting of not drinking when driving, and will applaud self-responsibility in this situation. It's much better to be completely sober when driving. Work out who will be the designated driver when you go out with friends.

In order to resist the peer pressure that you may experience, it is important to have made up your mind beforehand as to where your limit is. So whether you are not drinking alcohol at all, or only having a few glasses, have this limit in your head. It will probably be easier if you substitute a non-alcoholic drink for an alcoholic one, rather than not drinking at all. So when others are buying rounds, ask for an orange juice, for example. If you have some good reasons for not drinking, then you can wheel them out when people ask you. To some degree, in order to reduce the peer pressure, you just need to keep seeing it as an individual choice. When it comes down to it, there is going to be only so much pressure put on you, and you need to be able to say no for longer than they exert pressure. It can be seen as a need to see what you are doing as right and correct for you. You are not stopping others from enjoying themselves. And you aren't stopping yourself from having a good time, either. You'll just be in a much better space in the morning.

If you make a decision before you go out that you will only have four drinks, and then drink water or juice after that, then you will be able to enjoy yourself much more. You'll be able to remember everything, you'll be able to make better decisions, and you'll be less likely to end up in trouble, as well as have better short and long-term health outcomes.

> One night after work Megan went to the local pub and drank four Harvey Wallbangers. After that, she was the drunkest she'd ever been. Everything was blurred, she couldn't walk straight, and couldn't talk straight either. She was by herself, and to get home she had to cross a main road. The next day, she had no recollection of how she crossed the road, but she managed to find her way home. When she got home she put herself to bed. The room was spinning around and around and she felt extremely sick. The following morning she had a blinding hangover. From this experience, Megan decided that she would only have a couple of

> drinks at any one sitting. Since that time she has kept to her decision pretty well, only having perhaps up to three glasses of wine at any one time. She has never been so drunk again.

TOBACCO

Nicotine is a very addictive drug. Smoking has many negative effects, and very few positives. Cigarette smoke contains over seventy carcinogens that may cause cancer, and damage to the heart and circulatory system. Lung cancer is a big possibility, as well as heart disease, and a number of respiratory diseases including emphysema. It not only affects the health of the smoker, but also of those around them. In this time of plain packaging in Australia there is possibly less peer pressure now to smoke than in the past. And there are fewer places where one can smoke in the public arena.

If you do smoke, then the faster you manage to quit, the better your health outcomes will be. The added bonus is the extra money you will have, which you can either save or spend on other, healthier things. The more times you try to quit, the more likely it is that you will be able to give it up for good. It is important to work out what issues you will have when quitting, and the best ways to deal with them.

WHEN YOU GIVE UP SMOKING

- Twelve hours after stopping, almost all nicotine is out of your system with most by-products gone within five days.
- After twenty-four hours, the level of carbon monoxide in your blood has dropped dramatically, meaning your body can take and use oxygen more efficiently.
- After two days, your senses of taste and smell start to return.
- After two months, blood flow to your hands and feet improves.
- After one year, your risk of heart disease rapidly drops.
- After ten years, your risk of lung cancer is halved (3).

When I was quitting smoking, I found that I needed to give myself permission to eat biscuits instead of doing the hand-to-mouth action that I had done when smoking. That was a fairly big thing for me. So there I was watching TV, scoffing biscuits by the packet. I did put on about seven kilos, but after a few months I went back to my original weight. I also found that reading was good, because it took my mind off any cravings and took me to another reality. You can work out the best strategies to get through the cravings and try different ones each time you try to quit, so that the best one may come about to use on the ultimate attempt. Once you can get past the first three days, then you can look forward to three months, then one year and then longer. You can reward yourself for doing a good job by saving up the money that you would have otherwise spent on cigarettes and spending it on something that is healthier, such as going to the movies, a dinner out, or some other treat that you would enjoy.

VAPING

Now that e-cigarettes are reasonably widely available, it is important to discuss the effects of this form of inhaling. With vaping, although you don't get all the additives that are in tobacco, there are still some very negative effects that may ensue. You may still be getting nicotine, which is a strong and addictive drug. What vaping appears to be about is still having the feeling that you are breathing something in and breathing it out. As a result, both flavours and colours are added to make it more of a pleasant experience. The issue is that although the additives are generally fine in the foods we eat, we do not know the effects of them when inhaled, and this could be very important. There is already some indication that some flavours are not risk-free and, in fact, cause negative effects on functioning. In Australia there is an ongoing investigation on the effect of the use of nicotine in vaping that began in 2017. Currently, it is illegal to vape with nicotine. Explore the situation in your area.

DRUGS

Illegal drugs, and many other legal dugs, are basically poisons and have both short term effects and long-term negative effects. Drugs are now much more readily available than they used to be, as well as more affordable. This is no reason to use them, since many of them have addictive qualities and a tendency to ruin one's life. Opioids, methamphetamines and crack cocaine are particularly bad in this respect. You don't need mind-altering substances to enjoy yourself. Make your decision to remain drug-free, maintain your will-power, and don't succumb to peer pressure. You will find that you have a much better life being drug-free than otherwise. There are also psychedelic drugs such as magic mushrooms, acid and LSD. The draw here is for more of a spiritual experience, but this is not always the actual effect. If you are interested in being well-informed about the effects of drugs then you can visit (4) for a complete run down.

PRESCRIPTION DRUGS

There appears to be an increasing addiction to over the counter painkillers and prescription drugs. Because these are opioids it can be very difficult to wean yourself off them. However, it is worth the effort and attempt. In the first instance there may be a good reason why they are prescribed. These are not a long-term solution, though, and it would be more helpful to just use them as a short term solution for acute pain. Once addicted, the drugs treat the psychological addiction, and may not even be all that useful in reducing the actual physical pain felt. In this case, the effectiveness of the drug is reduced.

Prescription drug addiction can creep up on you, so it is worthwhile to take stock every now and then of your health and what you are taking. If you notice that you are ingesting a lot of tablets every day over a period of time, then you can take charge of your habit and do something about it. If you have chronic pain then there are other options that could be tried, such as hypnosis. Attendance at a pain clinic may also be helpful. St Vincent's Hospital in Sydney has an online chronic pain program too (5).

One particularly bad prescription drug that is currently being abused is Fentanyl. There is a high death rate among users, as the actual amount of the drug that is being consumed is unknowable. It is a very powerful painkiller and should not be taken recreationally. Because there is such a high risk of overdose, stay away from it.

PORNOGRAPHY

Most pornography is degrading, and watching it could easily give you the wrong ideas about what other people really want when it comes to sex. It is not only degrading, but it often shows violence or abuse, and this is just not right. It is much better if sexual partners can be on an equal footing with each other and enjoy the act of sex as individuals. Pornography may twist your beliefs about what sex should be like and what people want. It could also affect your future desires, and so it is best kept to a minimum or avoided altogether.

GAMBLING

Where you have experienced watching betting odds and betting advertisements over time, then you are more likely to have the attitude that betting is OK and everyone does it, so it's OK for you to do it too. This is not true. Not everyone is involved in betting. The consequences of betting on sports games can be just the thin edge of the wedge. It can lead to gambling addiction and gambling on a larger scale. It might be that you get yourself embroiled in gambling, so that it is difficult to stop, at which point it becomes an addiction. It is not too great a step from placing the occasional bet to becoming a problem gambler. People who are problem gamblers hold a set of beliefs about gambling that ensure their continuation of the problem behaviour. They believe that winning is likely, that they can win back the money they have lost, and that there are superstitions that will work to help them win. None of these really hold up when looked at closely.

Whether it's pokies, races, horses, sports games, scratchies or any form of gambling, the winners are not the punters. The winners are those who organise the betting. The odds always add up to be less than one. If it was 1.0 then it would be fairer, but the organisers make it less than one so that they make profits on that margin. Then the betting agents win overall. You, as a punter, do not win. The chances, or odds, of winning are miniscule in comparison to the likelihood of losing. Just because you have fed a lot of money into a betting game doesn't mean that the chances of winning now become any greater. For each game the odds are the same and the chances are new for that game. No superstitions actually work, whether it is playing a certain machine, or particular barrier numbers or wearing a lucky hat or anything of that nature. The odds are still the same, and the chances are that you will lose.

That gambling is addictive for a percentage of people is a fact, and there are many problem gamblers that have ruined their lives through chasing their losses and not getting help for their problem. Gambling is, on one level, a means to escape reality by getting into a zone of excitement and hope. This does not have positive consequences. Problem gamblers have lost their homes, lost their families, and may end up with huge debts, or possibly even in gaol. As with any addiction, if you become a problem gambler you can ruin your own life and also the lives of people you love.

You can stop yourself from going down that path if you acknowledge and accept your problem and get help from a counsellor or psychologist. There are also some specialist gambling services available. It is necessary to make the effort and ask for help, because it is extremely difficult to do it on your own. You don't need to do it by yourself. Get support.

SOCIAL MEDIA

Another possible addiction that you may not be aware of is an addiction to being online and on social media. It is a good thing if you are not welded to your mobile phone. See if you can refrain from checking it for a few hours. There are now new anxieties coming to the fore that include the fear of missing out on social media updates (FOMO). Why not check yourself to see whether you are addicted or not? Time yourself between your mobile checks. If it's less than five minutes then you may have FOMO (6). See how long you can go between checks, and notice if you become anxious or feel compelled to check your phone.

It is a fact that your world is not all online. See if you can reduce the online percentage and make a greater percentage of your time 'in person' and not online. See if you can leave your phone outside of your bedroom when you sleep. This will help you to not give in to any urges to check your phone, and the light will not keep you awake. You will also sleep better if you don't engage in any screen behaviour for at least one hour before you go to bed.

There are many platforms for social media nowadays. It is often a fun way to connect with friends. However, it is not the only way of connecting, and it is not the be all and end all that you might believe it to be. If you are a heavy user of social media and are continually connected then you can think about what else you do in your day. In order to live your life you should really live in the real world, not in the online world. It is important to discern the difference. Put more weight and value on the real friends that you have found from school, uni and work – the ones you go out with, the one's you can talk with, who will support you and who you have things in common with.

The online world is a very unforgiving world where people are faceless and can say anything. This can range from not including you in conversations or groups, to engaging in bullying behaviour. Disengage yourself to some extent from your online world. Bring yourself more into what you can hear, touch, feel and taste. Involve yourself more in the real world. Do it gradually. For a start, reduce the amount of time you are online. This might take a bit of getting used to, but you can do it. Gradually reduce the time until you are only checking on social media every hour instead of every five to ten minutes. Then you can reduce it even more, to every two hours or even longer. You could leave your phone in your bedroom while you sit outside in the sun, or while you are eating with your family. Your family will thank you for this. Think about the effect that your constant checking is having on your family relationships. Your family is likely to be feeling that you are distancing yourself from them, and putting them last. It can create ruptures in relationships. The most important connections that we have are to other people in real time, in the flesh; not to mobile phones. Build your connections with others in real time in person. This is what really matters. You don't need to be connected to social media all the time. You can just check in a few times a day.

GAMING

Gaming may have some positive attributes, such as increasing one's skill in the abilities the game requires, increasing reaction times, and concentration on the game. However, there are some drawbacks should you become addicted to playing. If you are spending a great deal of time on gaming, then you are not spending time on your relationships and daily living in the real world. Relationships may suffer, communication with others in general may suffer, and if you only focus on gaming, then your life is not going to get anywhere, and you will not grow within yourself as a person. While there is the possibility of associating with other gamers online, it is a very narrow and focussed world. It is more an escape from the real world than anything else. Once in a relationship, if gaming is occurring, then the relationship may break down unless the gaming time is curtailed.

See if you can limit the amount of time you spend gaming. Wean yourself off spending hours on it. Cut it down to one or two hours only a day, or even just once or twice a week, and you'll be able to spend some time with your friends and family, find employment, as well as having some leisure time not gaming. The older you are the less time you should be spending gaming, because it is likely that the responsibilities you have will be greater, and you need to look after the needs of yourself as well as those of others in your life.

SEX

A small percentage of people become addicted to sex. There is a difference between just being into sex and doing it a lot because of rampant hormones, and being addicted. While sex addiction can only be diagnosed and treated by a trained professional, some of the symptoms include feeling that sexual behaviour is difficult to control, often feeling ashamed of such behaviour, having difficulties with intimate relationships or with a known sexual partner, having legal problems due to sexual behaviour, hiding sexual behaviour from others, and having difficulties with work, school or social life due to sexual behaviour (7).

There is a tendency to prefer strangers over known partners. However, this does not mean that just because you have had a number of one-night stands that you are necessarily addicted to sex. There are a number of aspects that need to hold true before such a diagnosis can be given. If you suspect that you may have an addiction to sex then it would be worth your while doing some research and finding a trained professional in this area. See the references for the link to test yourself (7).

A SELF-CHANGE PROGRAM TO FREE YOURSELF FROM YOUR ADDICTION

With addiction there is often a physical component and a psychological component. Some substances have very difficult and potentially dangerous symptoms to manage when withdrawing.

In this instance, do some research before you stop and also seek professional help. It may be that a drug addiction centre is the best place to withdraw from the addiction. In any case, it is helpful to be armed with as much information as you need to start the process. Work out what you will do for the withdrawal symptoms. Both the physical and psychological. Take care to use non-addictive substances to replace the addiction.

Once you have worked out your strategies, and have perhaps engaged in some counselling to help motivate you, you can start. Monitor how you go if, for instance, you are cutting down on cigarettes. Keep on rewarding yourself as you go throughout the day. Reward yourself verbally. Encourage yourself. After a few days you could reward yourself by buying a small gift that has positive meaning for you. You could put the money you are saving towards a meal out, for example, or a movie night.

When overcoming addiction:

- Prepare – get information on withdrawal symptoms and how to manage them
- Commit to the change
- Work out strategies you can use to reduce discomfort
- Where appropriate avoid situations that may be triggers
- Have some counselling in this process
- Make a plan for management
- Monitor how you go and keep a record
- Put a reward system into place
- Usually, the more times you try to quit the more likely you are to succeed
- Use positive self-talk to encourage yourself
- Keep on visiting the reasons why you are quitting – keep renewing your commitment
- Reward yourself for positive movement
- Don't give up on quitting

BECOMING AWESOME

- Recognise that you have an addiction and then try to do something about alleviating the harmful effects.
- Seek treatment from a trained professional, whether psychologist or medical professional.
- Engage in stopping the addiction by yourself, if this is appropriate to your addiction. You would still need to do some research on how to go about this process and the best ways to do so.
- Work toward the goal of feeling more complete without having aspects of your life in difficulty.
- By taking these steps, you can become awesome at overcoming and avoiding addictions.

Chapter 12

Self-Esteem

When we are born we are perfect little human beings, no matter what (1). As we grow up we get told how we are. We tell ourselves how we are. There are pressures brought to bear on our perceptions of ourselves. If we get positive feedback from others more than negative feedback then we are likely to have a more positive perception of ourselves than negative. If this is the case then your self-esteem, your belief about yourself, will be quite high. On the other hand, if you get more negative feedback from others and you take that on board, then you will have lower self-esteem.

Sometimes, positive role models can make positive impacts on self-esteem.

When May was young her mother always put her down and so she believed she was useless. However, she had an aunt who was a role model for her and she was her

> saviour. May's aunt loved her and gave her unconditional supportive love. This helped May to believe in herself more. Further down the track, after May reached adulthood, she was able to draw on that belief in herself and breach some glass ceilings in her career.

If you don't really believe in yourself, or have positive thoughts about yourself, then you are more likely to be passive in your relationships with others, as well as having lower self-esteem. You are also unlikely to accept compliments about how you look and how you are as a person. Everything is coloured by low self-esteem. If you tend to be passive, then the best way to overcome your issues and to develop yourself is to work on improving your self-esteem, and then work on improving assertiveness. You will find it easier to stand up for yourself and to be assertive after you feel better about yourself and believe that you deserve to be treated better. However, it is not just being passive that may indicate low self-esteem. You may have low self-esteem and also be aggressive in your communication style. It can go either way. The answer for both is to work on building your self-esteem, and then work on assertiveness.

SITUATIONAL CONSEQUENCES

As we grow up we gain a sense of self, and it's the interaction between the self and the world, including the feedback we get, that determines how we see ourselves. If we get told lots of times that we are no good then that's what we will think about ourselves. This situation would lead to low self-esteem. Where we can master a number of skills then we might see ourselves as fairly competent in some things. Self-esteem is, to some extent, attached to other self-beliefs, such as competence. Such core beliefs rely on an individual's capacity to be willing to try new things and to keep on trying until mastery occurs. Some people are more likely to do this than others. Those who tend to give up early may have low self-esteem. This may be the case when people are older than children. It is when children are young that they stick at things like walking and talking until they have mastered them. Once these things have been mastered, there are many other things to try.

EFFECTS ON SELF-ESTEEM

Praise helps self-esteem to grow, while criticism causes it to fall. While it is not as cut and dried as this, this is a general rule that can be applied. However, it is not just what others say, although this is very important. It is also what you say to yourself in your self-talk that has an impact. At some stage as we grow up we take what others have said and we form an opinion about ourselves. Then we may tell ourselves negative things, in a sense we take over others' roles. If you agree with the criticisms you have received, then you will criticise yourself. The younger you are when you receive these criticisms, the more likely you will be to accept them. It does also depend on who is making the criticisms. The closer the relationship, the more impact it will have. If you have a good reason to disbelieve it then you will not be as affected by it. It is the importance to you of the source of praise or criticism as to whether you see it as deserved or not.

Some people tend to be innately more adventurous than others. There is also an innate tendency for extroversion or introversion (2). These are connected. In general, the more timid and introverted people are more likely to end up with lower self-esteem because when they compare themselves with others, they find themselves lacking to some extent. Other factors, such as parental encouragement and praise, may help to override this.

The important aspect is that a number of factors feed into self-esteem, and it changes throughout one's life depending on circumstances and situations that occur. One important factor is your self-talk. Another is praise and compliments. Another factor is criticism. If you are criticised over a period of time then your self-talk may not be able to compensate, and your self-esteem may go down as a result. This process occurs in bullying. If you are in your teens when this happens it may be worse in its effect, since the peer group is especially important at this time. However, bullying at any age is the wrong thing to do to anyone. It is a very negative experience to be the victim of it and can have dire consequences. The important thing to do is to tell people in a position of authority, such as parents, teachers, managers or employers. They may have some actions they can take to stop it or alleviate it in some way.

IMPROVING SELF-TALK

Your self-talk can have a great impact on your self-esteem. If you say the right things to yourself you can even improve your level of self-esteem. One way to improve self-esteem is by doing mirror work, as suggested by Louise Hay (1). You look at yourself in a mirror, meet your eyes and say out loud to yourself, I love you (your name). Say it as though you mean it, even if you don't believe it yet. Say it a number of times to get into the reality of it. Then you can find a good sentence that you can repeat to yourself as an affirmation. You need to repeat it at least twenty times a day. Out loud is good, but at least whisper it to yourself. The more you repeat it to yourself the more you can believe it, and your unconscious will be able to pick it up and run with it after a time. The first step is to do it consciously. It might take a month or so until it becomes easier to believe it and to think it, so stick with it. It might be a sentence such as:

I love and approve of myself.
I love myself just as I am.

You can start with something small, an affirmation that you can quite easily believe, and after a time you will internalise it. Once you have come to truly believe the affirmation, you can begin a new affirmation. Continue each affirmation for at least a month and notice the changes in your thinking over that time. Work up to saying that you love yourself. Since you were a tiny baby you deserved the love of others and you were perfect in every way. You have also deserved to love yourself since you were that tiny baby. This love is not arrogance, being up yourself, or narcissistic. It is just a love that you give to yourself, as you would give love to another human being. A love that is kind and gentle, that is forgiving and encouraging. You need to do these things for yourself most of all. You are perfect as you are. It is important for you to accept yourself, no matter what you see as your faults. Faults are not real. They are socially engineered and therefore they can go out of your reality and be forgotten. You are not just your body, you are more than your body. Similarly, you are not your behaviour, you are more than your behaviour. You are not your thoughts, you are more than your thoughts. You are not your beliefs, you are more than your beliefs. And so on.

EVOLUTION

You are as you are now, but 'now' changes, and as time passes you will grow and become transformed into the future you. You will have experiences that you learn from. You are not static, but continually evolving. Just for now, forgive yourself for any mistakes you make and learn from them. Do things differently. There is no point in beating yourself up about them. Do something different the next time. Accept yourself in your entirety and love yourself.

PATTERNS OF BEHAVIOUR

If your self-esteem is low then a number of behavioural patterns may show themselves. You may be more likely to reject compliments by commenting that you don't deserve it or don't believe it or otherwise somehow putting the compliment down. Instead, try saying, 'Thank you' and accepting it.

You may be more likely to get defensive easily and to take things personally when the other person may be just stating a fact about what happened. If you find yourself doing this then see if you can reduce your defensive stance and accept the facts.

Perhaps you don't really need to justify yourself. The other person is probably not attacking you and your role.

You are more likely to pay attention to other's needs instead of your own. You can also play on this by acting the martyr. This may get you brownie points if others acknowledge your selflessness, but only maybe. If you do it too much others may get sick of it or end up taking you for granted. In the end, this game doesn't really stack up as being useful. And it's a game you shouldn't need to play.

Another reason is that you become overwhelmed when the spotlight is on you. Self-consciousness may be an issue for you. This may be because you tend to be self-effacing and try to give others the credit when it's not necessarily warranted. If you give away your personal power like this then you could change your behaviour and allow yourself to see that you are worthwhile, as well as powerful, in your own right.

TURNING TO A MORE POSITIVE ASPECT

Improve your self-esteem at least to a level of being able to accept compliments and not reject them. Hopefully, this level will also mean that you believe that you love yourself and accept yourself. If you are not at this level then work on it until you are. You might just need to spend a little longer on your affirmations.

When you believe and accept the statement, 'I love and approve of myself as I am' then it should be easier to manage relationships with others. The first step is to improve the relationship you have with yourself, so once you have done this, relationships with others can be highlighted. When you know that you are OK then certain things follow. You understand that you deserve to be treated well, you can share things with others equally, and you can allow yourself to have some 'me time'. Additionally, you can allow your needs to be met, and ask others to help or to contribute. You can use the word 'I' in a sentence, and you are more able to stand up for yourself. The latter is why it is recommended that you work on improving self-esteem before you work on improving assertiveness. If you do it the other way around, it won't work as easily and you may find that you just get criticised for trying, and then you might go into a downward spiral.

POSITIVE SELF-ESTEEM

Where you have a built a reasonable level of self-esteem then you are more likely to see yourself in a positive light in a number of areas. For example, you will be able to assess realistically your competence in performing a variety of different tasks. You will also be more realistic in your assessment of the standards you expect, for yourself and others, as well as your safety concerns, and your ability to trust others. You will also take a more realistic view when assessing situations as they arise in daily life. As your feelings about yourself improve, you will be much more willing to speak your mind when you are in a situation that calls for this. All of these things are core beliefs, and they include self-esteem. If your core beliefs are generally higher then you will be a lot better off in many circumstances (3).

You can complete a rating system of your core beliefs. If you do complete it both before you work on your self-esteem and afterwards as well, then you will get a good idea of where you are at and how far you have moved between each completion. See the reference section for the link (4).

If you have medium self-esteem, whether by improving low self-esteem or otherwise, then a number of things follow:
- You are able to take compliments just by saying 'Thank you'.
- You are able to remain calm and focus on the problem when another person asks you questions about an issue rather than becoming defensive and taking it personally.
- You are able to accept that you have needs, and that you'd like them to be filled/met.

- You are able to be assertive and take your needs, as well as others' needs, into account.
- You are able to look after yourself better by taking care of yourself. If you are tired then you can say. 'No' to an outing and go to bed early.
- You can schedule self-care acts that will benefit you firstly, and others secondly. You look after yourself so that you can take care of others and dependents better.
- You are able to communicate your ideas to others in a manner that helps others to understand what you are saying. You do not need to play games to get one up on anyone else. Your communication is clear and direct.
- You are willing to grow in yourself and your skills. Self-development doesn't scare you. You are able to stretch your personal boundaries in relation to becoming a better you.
- You are happy getting feedback from others since it tells you how you are growing.

- You are able to see yourself as loveable, so do not have to prove anything to anyone.
- You are able to have an equal relationship and negotiate agreements you make and keep them going.
- Because you love yourself you expect good things to happen, instead of living in fear and not trusting others.
- You can be realistic in your expectations of yourself and others.
- As you love yourself you can be more forgiving of yourself and also of others.

Everyone is human and we all make mistakes. We can learn from our mistakes. Mistakes are, after all, just feedback.

Suffice it to say that having at least a medium level of self-esteem can change your life in many ways. The major way is in your communication with people. Since we are social creatures this can be a really huge change. It can touch all areas of your life for the better. So it makes it worthwhile to work on improving your self-esteem, doesn't it?

SELF-ASSESSMENT

When you are gathering evidence of who you are with others, it is important to give more weight to 'in the flesh' encounters. If you can manage it, reduce the importance of who you are online. Count both inwards and outwards communication. Give each type of behaviour a score between one and ten for how important it is as an indication of who you are.

Online behaviour can be seen as a way of interacting that is a means to an end. As with all interactions, it's good to be mindful of your needs as well as others. However, it may be the case that you have friends online that you will never meet. So keep a perspective on your online interactions that will enable you to distance yourself from how people behave online. And don't count it in your self-esteem assessment.

When looking at your life to get a sense of yourself and your self-esteem, count your family, friends, education, and see how you are in relationships – both close and not so close. You can assess how you feel about yourself in relation to your relationships and your abilities in general. Self-esteem is the overall feeling you have about yourself – just as you are.

While you may have self-confidence in your ability to do certain things and to behave in certain ways, being good at specific skills that may have particular importance to you also feeds into your self-esteem. However, if you have low self-esteem, you may discount your abilities and skills. Your abilities and skills also feed into your feelings of self-competence.

If you assess yourself as having medium to high self-esteem, that is positive. If you assess that you have low self-esteem then you can do the mirror work and affirmations. Another way of changing your beliefs is to engage in NLP and Time Line Therapy™ with a qualified NLP practitioner. There are other therapies that may help change beliefs that you can research.

You can seek out a qualified practitioner of your choice.

BECOMING AWESOME

- Work on improving your self-esteem.
- Think well of yourself through affirmations and mirror work, by changing what you say to yourself every day, or by another method that works for you.
- Keep working towards achieve new feelings until you make the change.
- Think of improving your self-esteem as paving the way to working on improving assertiveness.
- Believe in yourself.
- By taking these steps, your self-esteem can become awesome.

Chapter 13

Assertiveness

The best way to manage communication with others is to ensure it is clear and clean. When communication is clear and clean it is likely that boundaries are being respected: both for oneself and others. Acting in an assertive manner treats the relationship as adult-adult and respects boundaries. It takes into account your needs as well as others' needs. Acting assertively is something you can practice and learn. As a first step however, work on increasing your self-esteem if this is low, and when you have completed this, you can work on increasing assertiveness.

COMMUNICATION

In any communication between two people each person brings to the situation their own personality, attitudes, beliefs, values and mindset. These may differ greatly from each other.

Additionally, there is the context of the communication and shared meanings of words, which may or may not be complete. There are, therefore, a number of ways in which a communication may be misunderstood. This is why it is important to use words that both of you understand, and to check with each other that the communication was interpreted correctly. People do make assumptions, and this fact can also make things unclear. In the long run, the fewer assumptions you make and the more you clarify your communication, the more likely it will be that you get your message across.

Communication is coloured by our own beliefs, attitudes, and issues. There may be a way that we say something in a particular tone of voice, for example, because it is an issue for us. It might be a big issue or it might be a small issue, but nonetheless we may bring it out every time a situation occurs. These sorts of circumstances may get in the way of communicating with another in a clean fashion.

How you have an effect on the way you communicate may be an obvious thing. However, there are three styles of communicating that we are concerning ourselves with here. These are aggressive, assertive and passive.

The aggressive style is often threatening and demanding. The aggressor tells the recipient what to do, and may use a loud or confrontational tone of voice or hostile language. It puts the recipient into a defensive mode and they may be likely to respond in a passive manner. Aggressive communicators attempt to force their views onto others.

Passive communicators generally agree to whatever is said and go along with whatever is arranged. Passive communicators do not stand up for themselves. They say yes a lot, and are likely to have low self-esteem.

These ways of communicating disregard the other person's needs (aggressive) or one's own needs (passive). They are two extremes. On the other hand, if you are assertive then you are taking your needs and others' needs into account. You are standing up for yourself but not blaming the other person. This is the ideal style of communication. When you have learned to be assertive instead of passive or aggressive then you will find that your relationships flourish, and as a bonus you get your needs met more often (1).

AGGRESSIVE STYLE

If you are aggressive in your style of communication then you are being threatening to others, or at least telling them what to do, how to be, or how to act. The outcome of such treatment is that the other person feels that any choice has been taken away from them. They feel discounted, disregarded and disrespected. Where you are usually aggressive and belligerent with others, the question to ask yourself is why you feel the need to do this to them? Have you realised how others may feel in response to your behaviour? If not, then take it on board now and decide to do something about it and change to a more assertive style. It may be that you have different communication styles in different contexts. For instance, you may be aggressive at work, but not at home or vice versa. It is best to be assertive across all situations.

PASSIVE STYLE

Where you have a passive style of communication then you are acquiescing to whatever others are telling you to do, asking you to do, or expecting you to do. You are likely to put yourself last on any list, so that your needs are rarely met. You always give yourself the burnt chop. You may also have low self-esteem. Women are more likely to be passive than men due to cultural expectations. It is possible that you are only passive in certain contexts, such as at work, or you may be passive overall. As you have grown up and become older, you may have learnt to become more assertive in more contexts.

ANGER MANAGEMENT

Anger problems may drive the aggressive communication style, so one thing to do is to get some help with how you manage your anger. A counsellor or psychologist can be useful here, as can be specific anger-management programs. Since we have seen that thoughts lead to emotions, if you become aware of your thoughts and change them, then you should be able to change your responses.

AGGRESSIVE EXAMPLE

Here are some examples of an aggressive communication style. It usually gives the relationship an unequal footing, since it relates to a parent/child relationship.

'Do this for me' or just 'Do this.'
'You must do it.'
'Do it or else.'
'You'll be docked if you do (or don't) do it.'

PASSIVE EXAMPLE

If someone is passive they agree with almost everything that is requested of them or that they are told to do. They often give themselves the least or put themselves last. Again, it is a child/parent relationship, in as much as the other is seen to be better, more worthy and more valued.

Passive communication styles:
'Yes, I can do that.'
'I'm used to doing that task, so I'll do it.'
'Yes, I'm happy to do anything.'
'Yes, OK.'

By working out when you are being aggressive and when you are being passive, you can then make a choice about whether you want to change your style. There are going to be times when being passive is appropriate. However, if you are neglecting your own needs and wishes then it is important to become more assertive. There may even be times when it is appropriate to speak in the aggressive style. Overall, being assertive rather than aggressive is better and more appropriate in most situations. It is going to depend on your relationship to the other person and the context of the situation. Sort out in your own mind how the communications make you feel. Where you become angry or feel put upon, then perhaps you can change your style to assertiveness.

BEING ASSERTIVE

Assertive communication takes your needs into account, as well as the needs of others. It is an adult/adult relationship. It is much better to treat others as adults, and then you are on an equal footing. In this way, communication becomes cleaner and less manipulative. In the process of being assertive you do not blame the other person. When you are being assertive you are attacking the problem behaviour and not the person, so the other person is less likely to become defensive. One of the main ways to be assertive is to use 'I statements'.

For example, when you are trying to get a child to clean up their room, you can use an 'I statement' such as. 'When I see a messy room then I feel frustrated. What I'd like to see is a tidy room, so that I can easily put your clothes away.'

Where you are asking your friend to stop putting you down, 'When I hear a put down I feel hurt and disappointed. What I'd like instead is to hear encouraging statements about myself and what I can do. This will make me feel more positive towards you.'

In these examples you are describing the behaviour and not accusing the other. You are attacking the specific behaviour and you are owning the issue, since you are making I statements. This makes it much easier for the other person to accept what you are saying and not get defensive and aggressive.

Resolution is more likely when using assertiveness than when using aggression.

Sentences that are useful to use when being assertive:

I feel _____

I want _____

What I would like is _____

Being assertive and using I statements is not always going to work. It really depends on the other person and how they take it. If they are particularly aggressive then it might not work, so you really need to pick your fights. If the other person is passive-aggressive then they might respond with something along the lines of, 'Well that's your feeling', as though it is wrong for you to have those feelings. What is important is to be honest, clear and direct, and attack the problem and not the person. Concentrate and focus on good alternatives and possible options in dealing with the situation. If you can think on your feet in the moment and keep on repeating the outcome you want then you may get somewhere. If this doesn't work then at least you tried, and you can try again with a different person or in a different situation. It may be that you haven't yet found the right words that will work with that particular person. Experimentation may be helpful. Work out some sentences away from the situation that you can say, and then you will be more prepared when you try again.

One thing that you can do to be assertive is to say no when you want to say no. There is no reason to say yes to things you don't want to do, be involved with or be associated with.

Even if it feels strange and weird, even if it isn't your normal behaviour, you can start saying no if that's what you want to do. No-one will think badly of you for doing so. They will accept it. People are able to choose, and 'no' is a choice. Accept that you have a choice and make the choice to say no if that's what you'd like to do. Your world will not collapse because you say no. By saying no you will be able to feel proud of yourself, and after saying it the first time you will be amazed that it becomes a lot easier to keep on saying no to things you don't want to do.

Once you get into the habit of saying no when you mean it, then you will feel more strength within yourself. It is a matter of setting boundaries, and paying attention to your needs and wants is a part of this.

SOME COMMON PROBLEMS

It is all very well to be amenable and to want to please others, but saying yes to everyone is not necessarily going to get you where you want to be. You are likely to get to a stage where you are resenting others for constantly calling on your time and efforts. You can easily end up not having time for yourself, and your needs will be lost in providing for everyone around you. When you realise you are at this point, if not before, you need to start saying no to some people and start meeting your own needs for a change.

People may be able to be assertive in one area but not in another. If you needed to stand up for yourself against your siblings, you may find it quite easy to be assertive with your family. However, this might not translate to your friends or your working environment. When you are with your friends it is important to have boundaries set for yourself which you do not cross. For example, you need to behave in ways that are responsible and within the law. You could set a boundary or rule for yourself that you won't drink more than four drinks or that you will be home by eleven o'clock at night if you have to get up for work the next morning.

ACTING ASSERTIVELY AT WORK

One area of life where it can be difficult to act assertively is at work. The expectation is that you will do what is requested of you or whatever you are told to do. As you are paid, you are being compensated for this process. Some people think that this means that they can't object to anything. However, just because you are being paid doesn't mean that you can't stand up for yourself, within reason. It may well be important that your boss knows that you are snowed under and cannot do what he/she is asking of you in the time being suggested. It may also be of interest to your boss to know how well you have done with a project or job, especially if he/she doesn't always get kept in the loop. At any work meetings it would also be important to speak up and put your viewpoint forward, particularly if you have a good idea that would be of benefit to your company. All these situations, and many others, will require you to step up to the plate and say what you think. By being able to be assertive, it will mean that others will listen to you and take notice of what you say. Others will then make an assessment of you that is positive. So clear personality out of the way and just be remembered for what you say in an assertive manner.

In the example of being snowed under and being asked to do yet another task, you could say, 'I'm sorry but I'm snowed under right now. I can do it, but not this week. I'll be able to do it next week.'

If your boss insists on a deadline for this week, you could say, 'I need to negotiate which projects or tasks I leave until next week then. I cannot do it all this week. Will it be reasonable if I extend the deadlines for the other tasks I am currently working on?'

If you have a negative response here then you need to up it a notch and repeat what you said the first time. It may be helpful to go into detail about where you are up to with each task you are working on. Either negotiate which ones are left until later, or negotiate the time frame required. It will depend, to some extent, on the reasonableness of your boss. In any case, you will feel better if you say no and negotiate your way out of it.

Where you are laden up with work and there is no way out of it, then there may be a co-worker who may be able to be delegated to help you. This would be a reasonable request. Where this is not an option, and you are being bullied as well, then it is important to find out your employer's policies on bullying and strategies on reporting this behaviour.

BULLYING

Bullying often occurs over time and includes being spoken to aggressively, being called names to your face or behind your back, being belittled in front of work colleagues, being harassed, or being made fun of by others so that you feel angry, upset, embarrassed, ashamed or any other negative emotion. It probably makes you fearful of going to work, being at work, and you may hate it but feel trapped. Each workplace is supposed to have a bullying policy, and a means of reporting it. Don't just take it lying down. You need to stand up and do something about it. Report it and find another job if you can do this. It may just be the impetus you need to find a better job and a better career path. You never know.

PASSIVE-AGGRESSIVE

Apart from passive, aggressive and assertive, there is also the possibility that some people may be passive-aggressive. This occurs when a person appears to be agreeing with you or supporting you, but they are actually behaving aggressively or undermining you. So an employer might agree that you can do a certain project and then make it so difficult that you can't do it properly – for example, 'Yes, I'd love you to be part of the team working on the proposal for the new account. I'll give you the figures so you can write everything up.' And then, 'Oh, I'm much too busy to find those figures until next week.' Or a person may appear to give you a compliment, but when you analyse it, they have actually insulted you – for example, 'I really like your shoes. It must be difficult to find something that looks good when you have such wide feet.'

TOTALLY ASSERTIVE

If you are practising being assertive, then you need to get the whole package right. It is not just about the words themselves but also how you say them, your body language, and so on (2).

Eye contact – practice looking the other person in the eyes to show sincerity.

Body posture – it's best to face the person, sit or stand appropriately close, and lean slightly towards them with head erect.

Gestures – gestures add extra emphasis. Suitable facial expressions show interest

Voice tone, volume – a level, well-modulated voice is convincing without being intimidating. No whispering or shouting.

Timing – sometimes it might be more appropriate to see the person privately.

Content – it is the interpretation of the words by the listener that will determine the response.

There is no hard and fast rule to omit the pronoun 'you'. It is, however, important to reduce the blaming aspect, so that you avoid saying things such as, 'You stopped me from leaving work on time last Friday, so I missed my doctor's appointment.' Or 'You made me burn the dinner.' If it is a positive statement then it is fine to use 'you'. Even in other circumstances it might be the only option to make sense of the sentence.

WHAT TO DO WHEN...

When you feel that people are behaving aggressively towards you, it may be best to ignore such behaviour. When you and the other person have both calmed down, then it may be appropriate to address the behaviour assertively. Initially, it is a good idea to delay your reaction and utilise positive self-talk, such as, 'Why should I let someone else's behaviour affect me?' and, 'Stay calm'.

It is helpful to rehearse future situations in your head or in real life, with a friend or in front of the mirror, for example. Work out what you want to say, how to say it and practice your tone of voice and firmness. Then it will be a lot easier to get it right at the time you need to say it. The more you actually carry out being assertive in various situations, the better you will be at doing it.

Assertion involves expressing appropriate feelings. Deciding whether an action is appropriate or not is a social judgement. However, it is best to implement the minimal effective response when it comes to feelings such as hurt or annoyance. For example, you might say to a waiter, 'I believe you have made an error in the bill. Would you mind checking it again?' (2, p75). In such circumstances don't assume that the mistake was deliberate. Don't, in fact, assume anything.

Being assertive is a good move. It helps you feel equal to others, and means that you are looking after yourself and others' needs. When you are assertive, communication is clean and respectful. Others will also respect you when you are assertive. They will take notice of you and your requests. You will find that you make a difference to your own life. This means that your self-esteem may also improve. Your self-beliefs are likely to increase in the area of competence as well. Overall, it is definitely worthwhile to work on becoming more assertive.

BECOMING AWESOME

- Work out your usual communication style, and work on becoming assertive in more situations.
- Ensure you use a calm and measured tone of voice and make requests rather than demands, if you are an aggressive communicator.
- Start saying no in situations that are not too difficult for you, if you are a passive communicator, then move on to saying no more often, until you are used to saying no.

- Start speaking up and using 'I statements'. Let others know what you really want.
- Make your communication clear and clean.
- By taking these steps, you can become awesome at being assertive and communicating with others.

Chapter 14

Personal Growth

Personal growth is a good thing. When we change, especially when we do this consciously, then this is personal growth. If you have increased your self-esteem and become more assertive, these are part of personal growth. Becoming more aware of your thoughts, feelings and behaviour is personal growth. Change is a constant in our lives. It is much better if you help to drive that change by becoming a better person, dealing with your issues and becoming more whole or complete. You will then become happier, and have the ability to make others happy too.

The first step to personal growth is to become aware that you *can* change yourself. Taking responsibility for actioning the change means that you take charge, and only you can do it. Then it is important to work out what it is that needs to change. Is it self-esteem, assertiveness, or something else, such as how you relate to others?

For a more detailed look at self-awareness and working out your issues, as well as goal setting, see my book *Setting Yourself Free (1).* You can work through the exercises in *Setting Yourself Free,* and continue your journey through *Creating an Awesome You.*

A couple of points to start with are that change occurs in the present moment, and it is better to spend the majority of your time in the present, rather than thinking about the past or worrying about the future. If you can do this then you will find many benefits, including increasing your happiness.

OUT OF YOUR COMFORT ZONE

At a particular moment in time we may have personal boundaries we don't cross. Boundaries are good to have, especially when it comes to personal behaviour in relation to others. You can also have boundaries for others in relation to their behaviour towards you (2). Boundaries for behaviour are different to those limitations you place on yourself to stay within your comfort zone. You can ask yourself what will stretch you in a positive sense, so that you can increase your comfort zone of skills, behaviours, or ways of being? What will cause you to grow? You could choose to do nothing and just let life throw you situations that you might grow from, or you could take the initiative and take action consciously. You might do a short course to improve your career options, or a leisure course such as pottery, learning a new language, or craftwork. Not only will you learn a new skill, but you will make new pathways in your brain. This is a good thing.

LEARNING MORE

If you decide to do a university course, investigate the career options that would eventuate. It is important that you are at least interested in the field you are looking to study within. If you aren't interested and can't see yourself working in that field, what would be the point of completing a degree? It's also helpful to have some talent or skill in something that is involved in the course, whether it is maths, science, or the arts.

OTHER STRETCHES

If you are not interested in attending a course of some description, then work out what you want to do. What would stretch you just enough to reach a new height?

If you recognise that you have some issues that need addressing before you can make a clear decision, then you could consider counselling with a psychologist or counsellor. You could also consider seeing an NLP practitioner. There are NLP techniques and Time Line Therapy™ techniques that are tailor-made for personal growth. Work out what you want to work on and make an informed choice regarding your practitioner. Make sure you ask them questions about their qualifications, whether they are supervised or have peer supervision, and also questions about their philosophy of working with you. You will be able to tell from their answers whether they will be a good fit for you. Spending money on your personal growth sessions will be a good investment, and you are worth it. We don't spend nearly as much as we should on our inner wellbeing, and doing so will be worth it in the long run. Additionally, it may even be worth it in the short term since your feeling of wellbeing is likely to increase once you have addressed the issues you want to address, and begun to make progress.

GOAL SETTING

It is good personal policy to set goals. You can then begin to take action to achieve them. Goals need to be SMART. That is specific, measurable, attainable, realistic, and time-famed. The goal needs to be: specific, so that you know it when you have reached it; measurable, so you can track your progress; attractive to you, so that you are motivated to reach it; realistic, so that you can actually achieve it; and time-framed, so that you can check your progress as you go and review your goal regularly. A time frame also helps you to take actions and steps towards your goal, so that you will achieve it in the time frame you have given yourself. For more on goal setting please see (3).

Goal theory has evolved today to include the fact that particular goals need to be approached differently. Goals are divided into two kinds. These are performance goals and learning goals. A performance goal is something that is fairly straightforward and can be measured directly in terms of output. A learning goal is something that you haven't done before, or don't know what the output will actually be. In this case, the only thing you can do is your best. The important aspect here is that you are trying out new behaviours and seeing what you can do, and eventually improving on your initial behaviours (4).

MAKING DECISIONS

When you have an important decision to make, it will be helpful to use the Decisional Balance (5). You divide an A4 page into quarters. You then label the columns as Change and Not Change, and the rows as Good and

Bad. Once you have done this, you make a list in each box. The top left will list the good things about the change you are considering. The top right will list the good things about not changing. The bottom left will list the bad things about changing and the bottom right will list the bad things about not changing. The good things about changing are the things that are motivating you to make the change. The bad things about not changing are the things that you want to avoid, they are the motivators away from where you currently are. The good things about not changing are the things that are blocking you and consist of your secondary gain.

Once you have had a fair amount of time thinking about these four lists, go through and rate each one out of ten, where ten is the most important. Once you have done this, look through the lists and you should be able to make a decision based on all this information. It is also important to think about your feelings about making the change, and what may eventuate. Hopefully you have considered these aspects in your lists. Once you have completed this task, you will know that you have done what you can to take all the information into account.

INTUITION

Everyone has intuition. The question is whether you take notice of it or not. Intuition is your gut feeling about a situation, although it can operate as a thought that comes into your mind already formed. It can be a bit difficult to work out what is a thought you had and what is intuition. Hindsight can be good in this case, to get a sense of which it was. You can teach yourself how you receive intuitions and then you can start to pay attention to your intuition more often. Should you do so, you will find that things may work out better and everything falls into place more easily.

How can you tell if your intuition is telling you something?

Sometimes it feels as though the thought just pops into your mind fully formed. It can also feel like a 'knowing'. It is certainly not happening when you are pondering over something and thinking it through, unless, in the process of doing so, you find a fully formed thought just pop into your mind from left field. However, don't let your desire for something get confused with your intuition, since intuition is often desire-free. It doesn't operate all the time, but the more you listen to it, the more it will occur. The ideas that occur to you from your intuition are not silly ideas, they are more about keeping you safe, getting the best out of your life, and helping others. It is a positive and life-affirming force that you can use to good ends.

> When Karen was twenty-two she got engaged to her long term partner, Tom. They were already living together, so it was a natural step to take. Once they had decided to get married, Tom went overseas for six weeks. After a couple of weeks, Karen went over and met him in Geneva. It was apparent that he was a bit disappointed to see her. She had a thought that the relationship wasn't right, but didn't listen to herself. They

came back from overseas, got married, and had three children. Even before the wedding, Karen knew that getting married was the wrong thing to do. However, she'd had such a difficult life up to that point that she wanted the stability and security of marriage, and fantasied about being part of a happy family. Although Karen wouldn't be without her children, the marriage was never a very happy one, and she often wonders how her life would have turned out if she had listened to her intuition.

OPTIMISM AND PESSIMISM

People differ in their expectations of the future. They have a tendency to be either optimistic or pessimistic. If you are optimistic then you see yourself and events in a generally positive light. If you are pessimistic then you see yourself and events as having more negative outcomes. While the pessimist may be more of a realist in thinking, it is the optimist who wins on all fronts.

Martin Seligman (6) has shown that optimists have better health, better relationships, greater tenacity, and, as a result, are more successful than pessimists. If you have identified yourself as a pessimist it is possible to train yourself to become more of an optimist in thinking, and if you do this, then you will gain from having this positive stance.

Pessimists tend to blame the outcome of an event on global, permanent and intrinsic (inside of oneself) factors. For instance, if a pessimist fails a test they might tell themselves it's because they're stupid. On the other, hand an optimist would tell themselves that they didn't do enough work for the test, making the explanation specific, temporary and extrinsic (outside of oneself).

You can practice optimism by explaining outcomes you achieve in terms of specific, temporary and extrinsic factors. You may need to consciously engage in this for a time before you are able to think like an optimist automatically. It will be helpful to use this style of explanation in terms of other's behaviours too, by giving others the benefit you are now giving yourself. Others will be happy with this situation, as they will feel supported. Overall, you will become more optimistic, but you may not change your tendency towards pessimism completely. More optimism is a lot better than none. You should find that your health improves, your resilience improves and your ability to bounce back from setbacks will also improve (6).

INTEGRATION

Dan Siegel (7) has an interesting theory of health and wellbeing. This has our brain and our mind as the central player. He talks specifically about mental and emotional health. In his model, integration is both the goal and desired present state. Human beings are complex systems, receiving input from outside themselves, and being able to self-organise. Emotions may lead people to states of rigidity or of chaos when dysfunction occurs. When impairment to emotional wellbeing occurs, the movement is away from the flow of integration to either rigidity or chaos. He puts the flow of integration like a river between the banks of rigidity and chaos. The river of integration is where harmony reigns and in this space people are able to be: Flexible, Adaptive, Coherent, Energised and Stable.

Sometimes we might move towards rigidity and feel stuck, or we might move towards chaos and feel that life is unpredictable and out of control. Being in the flow allows us to live moment-to-moment, taking things as they happen and letting life unfold. According to Siegel there are eight domains of integration. These are: the integration of consciousness, horizontal integration, vertical integration, memory integration, narrative integration, interpersonal integration, and temporal integration. Integration can become blocked as a result of developmental difficulties or other life experiences. Any of these domains can become blocked, and problems or issues may arise.

Another concept is that of 'mindsight'. It is mindsight that can help us back to integration. Mindsight is a kind of self-awareness which involves observation, objectivity and openness. This is a process can be done with the help of a psychologist or counsellor, if not by oneself. Sometimes it is difficult to separate out the steps needed and the processes that will take you back to integration without outside help. One way to do it alone is through engaging in mindfulness.

Mindfulness is a process that focuses attention on moment-to-moment experience (7). By changing the focus of attention to this on a regular basis you may be changing your brain. In mindfulness you are getting your brain to be mentally active, and this trains your mind to become aware of awareness itself, and to pay attention to your own intention. In this way, you become aware of being aware and you are able to take that step back and observe yourself in the present moment in a non-judgemental manner.

To exercise mindfulness, close your eyes and focus on your breath. Letting your awareness be on your breathing, breath in and breath out. If you become lost in a memory or thought, when you realise that this is happening, let that thought go and return the focus to your breathing. Just focus on being aware of being aware and being in the moment. Start off with five minutes daily and work up to ten minutes. The more you do it, the easier it gets and, after some time, you will be more at peace with your world. Do it alone or find a class in your area.

POSITIVE PSYCHOLOGY

Since around 2002, Martin Seligman has been involved in devising and furthering his theory of positive psychology (8). Although undergoing some changes, he now proposes that wellbeing theory is at the heart of positive psychology. Wellbeing has five measurable elements that contribute towards it. They are:

- Positive emotion – such as happiness.
- Engagement – learning new things, and being in the flow.
- Relationships – that are more positive than negative.
- Meaning – that you attach to what you do.

- Achievement – achieving things for the sake of it.

If you have all these elements and they are positive rather than negative, then you are flourishing (8).

In *Flourish* (8), a number of exercises are suggested that will help to improve your wellbeing. Have a think and see if you would like to engage in any of the following exercises.

GRATITUDE GIFT

Remember someone who is still alive who did something or said something which changed your life in a positive direction. When we express gratitude to others, we actually strengthen our relationship with them. Your task is to contact this person and say that you would like to do something for them as a gift in return for what they did for you. Your gift might be to do some gardening, bake them a cake, take them shopping, or just buy them a present and give it to them. As part of your gift, tell them how what they did impacted your life in a positive way and what the outcome is. Then discuss this and your feelings for one another. Doing this will hopefully help you to feel happier.

WHAT WENT WELL

This one follows the idea of focussing on what you want, rather than on what you don't want. What we focus on is where our attention goes.

In this exercise, at the end of the day for at least a week, write down one positive thing that happened during the day. Also write why it happened. An example might be that you had a good conversation with a friend. The 'why' might be because she is a kind and thoughtful person. In the second week, write down two things that went well each day, and why. In the third week find three things that went well each day, and why. You will find that you are looking for positive events more often and you'll be able to remember them better. Consequently, you will start to feel happier. Sometimes this can be a challenging exercise, because usually we are looking out for the negatives. However, you will find that persistence pays off.

The positive psychology exercises should help you to feel better, happier, and end up with a greater feeling of wellbeing. In our lives we tend to like to feel that we are moving forward rather than feeling stuck and not getting anywhere. These exercises should help you to feel you are getting somewhere. It doesn't necessarily matter where you are going, it just matters that you are in the process of moving forward. This feeling of moving forward is, in fact, growth. Personal growth can be intentional or it might be incidental. As you grow you change, and as the days pass you grow and perhaps change in a myriad of small ways, so that after a year you might notice the differences. It might be that you have decided to do something differently, or even a few things, or perhaps you feel differently about something or someone. It doesn't matter how small the change is, it is still a change, and it may be termed growth.

Growth may occur through just living, particularly if you go along with it. Personal growth can be hurried up by engaging in activities such as learning new things, and this will mean that the graph of your personal growth will rise exponentially. This is positive for you. It is exciting to learn new things, and achieving this learning will, as we have seen in wellbeing theory, enhance your wellbeing. Plan to engage in an activity every year that will stretch you to some degree, whether it stretches your skills, your mind or your body, in terms of becoming more fit. Of course, it is helpful to keep your risk down, so do what is safe.

Stretch yourself just a bit, so that you are increasing some capability that you have. Every time you increase your beliefs about your capacity to do something, your belief about you as a person improves too, or at least your belief about yourself as being competent improves. So you are working on your beliefs about yourself as well as your skill set. The more you find out about yourself in your self-discovery journey the better. Finding out where your limits are is still self-discovery. You can become more self-aware by working on being present in the moment, just as Alice did.

> After suffering concussion, Alice's doctor advised that to heal herself she needed to stop over-thinking.
>
> She found it hard to understand this, and was told that she needed to be in the 'now'. This idea was completely foreign to her. She struggled for months, trying to understand the 'now' and to cease her thinking. She would constantly catch herself in mind chatter. She became frustrated by her actions, so would start yelling at herself to cease the activity in her mind. In addition, she started to observe her behaviour. She realised she couldn't admire the ocean without getting bored, but could easily get distracted by technology.
>
> This is when her journey to understand the workings of the mind and the 'now' began. During her research, she came across a concept of giving 'no reality' to anything that caused agitation. The instruction was simple: all one needs to do is repeat, 'I am not giving this any reality.'

She immediately started trialling this on herself and her family. Each time she felt any annoyance, she would repeat, 'I am not giving this any reality.'

As she applied this practice, she realised she was calmer, and finally experiencing the 'now', rather than being reactive, which had only ever resulted in her either becoming lost in thought or caught in an argument.

Her family and friends now also apply the practice of telling themselves, 'I am not giving this any reality.'

SELF-DISCOVERY

Where there are limits to your skills in one direction that does not rule out going in another direction. However, it is important to be realistic. Where you find you do not have any particular talent in sport, then explore things to do with your mind. Learn things, learn a language, or learn something else you have an interest in. It is all grist for the mill. Where you like words and are good at English then perhaps you could put your mind to creating a story, or you could write a blog about something that interests you. Be creative!

In your journey of self-discovery it might be easier to work on obvious things first. This means that if you have a self-esteem issue then work on this first, followed by assertiveness, followed by whatever other issue you have. Once you have worked through your issues, you can expand your horizons and work on improvement. Improve your relationships, then improve your skills and capabilities. Personal growth can be constant. It can be a constant source of happiness and achievement. Making you and your life better may be a lifelong goal, which you can continually achieve.

How you do things and what you do needs to be in line with the real you. You need to be true to yourself. It is OK to be inspired by the positive qualities that other people have, but comparing yourself in a way that makes you feel superior or inferior is never helpful to our relationship with ourselves or our relationships with others.

SELF-COMPASSION

When it comes to criticism we are often the hardest on ourselves. We may tell ourselves off and beat ourselves up over things we have said, done or thought. Your self-talk is very important, and if a lot of it is negative then you are likely to have negative feelings about yourself a lot of the time. It is important to be self-compassionate. You should extend to yourself the forgiveness and kindness that you would give to a friend or family member in the same situation. The more kind you can be to yourself, and the more positive self-talk you give yourself, the better. The Losada ratio also holds for your self-talk. So be kind to yourself.

BECOMING AWESOME

- Set yourself a goal every year to engage in self-development. This will hasten the process of your growth as a human being.
- Work on your issues first, followed by improving your life in other ways, whether working on

communication and relationships or learning new things.
- You can improve your wellbeing through the suggested exercises.
- Engage in activities that expand your comfort zone and stretch you.
- By taking these steps, your self-development can be awesome.

References

CHAPTER 2

1. P.D. Gluckman. P Hofman. & M.A. Hanson (2005). The fetal, neonatal, and infant environments—the long-term consequences for disease risk. Early *Human Development,* Volume 81, Issue 1, January 2005, Pages 51-59.
2. The Diet Testers. SBS TV program, 19/4/2018.
3. IARC (2015) The International Agency for Research on Cancer (IARC) has classified processed meat as a carcinogen, something that causes cancer. And it has classified red meat as a probable carcinogen, something that probably causes cancer. IARC is the cancer agency of the World Health Organization. https://www.cancer.org/latest-news/world-health-organization-says-processed-meat-causes-cancer.html. Accessed online 11/6/17.

4. Wikepedia, Veganism. https://en.wikipedia.org/wiki/Veganism. Accessed online 7/6/18
5. Jacka et al (2017) BMC Medicine. www.deakin.edu.au/about-deakin/media-releases/articles/world-first-trial-shows-improving-diet-can-treat-major-depression. Accessed online 11/6/17
6. Salas-Salvado J, et al. Reduction in the Incidence of Type 2 Diabetes With the Mediterranean Diet: Results of the PREDIMEDReus nutrition intervention randomized trial. *Diabetes Care*, 2011.
7. Estruch R, et al. Effects of a Mediterranean-Style Diet on Cardiovascular Risk Factors. *Annals of Internal medicine*, 2006.
8. Estruch R, et al. Primary Prevention of Cardiovascular Disease with a Mediterranean Diet. *The New England Journal of Medicine*, 2013.
9. CSIRO (2005) *The CSIRO total wellbeing diet.* Penguin Books. Australia.

10. Nutrition Australia (2017). http://www.nutritionaustralia.org/national/resource/healthy-living-pyramid. Accessed online 11/6/17.
11. Good Sleeping Habits at https://www.healthdirect.gov.au/healthy-sleep-habits. Accessed online 1/6/18.
12. (2013) http://www.earthcalm.com/having-trouble-sleeping-may-be-an-emf-health-effect. Accessed online 19/6/17.
13. https://www.activebeat.co/your-health/6-health-problems-associated-with-too-much-sleep/5/. Accessed online 30/3/18.
14. *Trust Me I'm a Doctor,* SBS, 2017.
15. *Ask The Doctor* TV program, channel 2, ABC (30th May, 2017).
16. *The Truth About Fasting.* SBS TV Program with Michael Moseley. 2016.
17. Min Wei, Sebastian Brandhorst, Mahshid Shelehchi, Hamed Mirzaei, Chia Wei Cheng, Julia Budniak, Susan Groshen, Wendy J. Mack, Esra Guen, Stefano Di

Biase, Pinchas Cohen, Todd E. Morgan, Tanya Dorff, Kurt Hong, Andreas Michalsen, Alessandro Laviano, Valter D. Longo. Fasting-mimicking diet and markers/risk factors for aging, diabetes, cancer, and cardiovascular disease. *Science Translational Medicine,* 2017; 9 (377): eaai8700 DOI: 10.1126/scitranslmed. aai8700. https://www.sciencedaily.com/releases/2017/02/170216103923.htm. Accessed online 21/4/18.

18. Appel. L. et al, (2013). https://www.thinkingnutrition.com.au/dietary-supplements-benefits/. Accessed online 11/6/17.

19. www.eatthis.com/foods-that-cause-inflammation. Accessed online 10/6/18.

20. www.health.havard.edu/staying-healthy/foods-that-fight-inflammation. Accessed online 10/6/18.

21. Dizpensa, J. (2014) *You are The Placebo: Making Your Mind Matter.* Hay House: USA.

22. Rankin, L. (2013) *Mind Over Medicine: Scientific Proof That*

You Can Heal Yourself. Hay House: USA.
23. WHO Guidelines (2016). https://www.google.com.au/?gws_rd=ssl#q=who+exercise+guidelines. Accessed online 11/6/17.
24. Mayo Clinic (2017) http://www.mayoclinic.org/healthy-lifestyle/fitness/in-depth/exercise/art-20048389. Accessed online 11/6/17.
25. *Trust Me I'm a Doctor,* SBS, 2017.
26. Michael Moseley The Truth About Getting Fit. ABC 17/7/2018.

CHAPTER 3

1. Corfield EC, Martin NG, Nyholt DR. (2017) Familiality and Heritability of Fatigue in an Australian Twin Sample. *Twin Res Hum Genet.* 2017 Jun; 20(3):208-215.
2. Bowlby (1969) *Attachment and Loss.* Penguin: UK.
3. Seligman, M.E.P. (1992) *Learned Optimism.* Random House: Australia.

4. Seligman, M.E.P. (1993) *What You Can Change ... And What You Can't.* Ballentine: USA.
5. McKay, M. & Fanning, P. (1991) *Prisoners of Belief.* New Harbinger: USA.
6. www.dianahutchison.com/shop
7. www.dianahutchison.com/shop
8. Elliott, (1970) *The Eye of the Storm.* ABC: USA. https://en.wikipedia.org/wiki/Jane_Elliott#First_exercise_involving_eye_color_and_brown_collars. Accessed online 12/6/17.

CHAPTER 4

1. https://mic.com/articles/106764/why-it-s-better-to-have-4-amazing-friends-than-400-just-ok-ones#.1AMk8HRHG. Accessed online 15/7/2018.
2. https://www.lifehacker.com.au/2018/03/this-is-how-many-friends-you-need-to-be-happy/. Accessed online 15/7/2018.
3. http://www.thisisinsider.com/being-best-friends-with-spouse-benefits

-2018-3. Accessed online 15/7/2018.
4. Bowlby (1969) *Attachment and Loss.* Penguin: UK.
5. Hughes, Dan (2013) *8 Keys to Building Your Best Relationships (8 Keys to Mental Health).* WW Norton & Company: New York.
6. Seligman, M.E.P. (1993) *What You Can Change ... And What You Can't.* Ballentine: USA
7. Boundaries. https://positivepsychologyprogram.com/great-self-care-setting-healthy-boundaries/#relation. Accessed online 18/2/18.
8. https://www.psychcentral.com/lib/what-are-personal-boundaries-how-do-I-get-some/. Accessed online 12/09/18.
9. Tartakovsky, M. (2016). 10 Way to Build and Preserve Better Boundaries. *Psych Central.* Retrieved on November 15, 2017, from https://psychcentral.com/lib/10-way-to-build-and-preserve-better-boundaries/
10. http://www.allprodad.com/10-ways-to-establish-clear-boundaries-for-children/. Accessed online

16/11/17. *Making Children Mind without losing yours* by Kevin Leman.
11. Seligman, M. (2011) *Flourish*. Random House: Australia.
12. Hutchison, D.E. (2018) *Setting Yourself Free*. 2nd ed. DoctorZed Publishing: Australia.

CHAPTER 5

1. Seligman, M.E.P. (1993) *What You Can Change ... And What You Can't.* Ballentine: USA.
2. Helplines For Australia:
   Kids Helpline: 1800 55 1800
   Headspace: www.headspace.org.au
   Lifeline: www.lifeline.org.au 13 11 14
   Wesley Mission: www.wesleymission.org.au Mental Health 1300 924 522.
   For sexual assault, domestic and family violence: 1800 737 732.
   For a complete list of helplines for Australia go to https://aifs.gov.au/cfca/publications/helplines-and-telephone-counselling-services.

CHAPTER 6

1. Australian Government Website for travellers: www.smarttraveller.gov.au

CHAPTER 7

1. Cairns, Julie Ann (2015) *The Abundance Code: How to Bust the 7 Money Myths for a Rich Life Now.* Hay House Inc.: US.
2. Hutchison, D.E. (2018) *Setting Yourself Free.* 2nd ed. DoctorZed Publishing: Australia. www.dianahutchison.com/shop
3. In Australia, one such ethical microfinance company is Good Shepherd Microfinance.
4. Moneysmart website: https://www.moneysmart.gov.au/managing-your-money/managing-debts/dealing-with-debt-collectors.
5. https://www.moneysmart.gov.au/scams.
6. https://afsa.gov.au/insolvency/i-can't-pay-my-debts/what-are-the-consequences-bankruptcy.

CHAPTER 8

1. Holland, J.L. (1988) *Self Directed Search.* Edited by Jan Lokan. Australian Edition. Adapted from the American SDS Published by Psychological Assessment Resources with permission. ACER.
2. www.truity.com/test/holland-code-careertest.
3. http://www.abc.net.au/news/2017-11-14/communication-interpersonal-skills-could-trump-stem-at-work/9148528. ABC article about future jobs. Accessed online 14/11/17.
4. www.fairworkhelp.com.au/Fair-Work/Ombudsman: 1300 856 110

CHAPTER 9

1. https://www.ourwatch.org.au/understanding-violence/facts-and-figures. Accessed online 15/7/2018.
2. Damasio AR. (1994). *Descartes' error: Emotion, reason, and the human brain.* New York, NY: Putnam.
3. www.dianahutchison.com/shop

4. Gendlin, E.T. (1981). *Focusing.* Bantam Books: USA.

CHAPTER 10

1. Butler, A.C., Chapman, J.E., Forman, E.M., & Beck, A.T. (2006). The empirical status of cognitive-behavioural therapy: A review of meta analyses. *Clinical Psychology Review,* 26, 17-31.
2. Jacka et al (2017) BMC Medicine. http://www.deakin.edu.au/about-deakin/media-releases/articles/world-first-trial-shows-improving-diet-can-treat-major-depression. Accessed online 11/6/17.
3. Worden, J.W. (2009) *Grief Counselling and grief therapy: A Handbook for the Mental Health Practitioner* (4th ed) New York: Springer Publishing.
4. APS (2017) https://www.headsup.org.au/docs/default-source/default-document-library/stress-and-wellbeing-in-australia-report.pdf?sfvrsn=7f08274d_4. Accessed online 1/8/18.

5. https://www.eatingdisorders.org.au/eating-disorders. Accessed online 21/4/18.
6. Miller, Caroline A (2014) *My Name is Caroline* (2nd Ed.) Cogent Publishing: USA.
7. https://nationaleatingdisorders.org/learn/by-eating-disorder/arfid. Accessed online 21/4/18.
8. https://www.eatingdisorders.org.au/eating-disorders/binge-eating-disorder?gclid=Cj0KCQiAzrTUBRCnARIsAL0mqczxTJC2xDyMLpKzVj97FINWTX3haJzGSnOSk1CNBXA1WZXYNiXMn6AaAgg1EALw_wcB. Accessed online 22/2/18.
9. http://www.orthorexia.com/ There is the authorised Bratman Orthorexia self test on this site. Accessed online 22/2/18.
10. See St Vincent's online social phobia program and other programs they offer, such as for depression, anxiety, chronic pain, mindfulness, and post-traumatic stress disorder. https://thiswayup.org.au/

11. Seligman, M.E.P. (1993) *What You Can Change ... And What You Can't.* Ballentine: USA.
12. Sane Australia (2017) https://www.sane.org/mental-health-and-illness/facts-and-guides/cannabis-and-psychotic-illness. Accessed online 19/6/17.

CHAPTER 11

1. SA Health (2016). http://www.sahealth.sa.gov.au/wps/wcm/connect/public+content/sa+health+internet/about+us/health+statistics/alcohol+and+drug+statistics/alcohol+use+statistics. Accessed online 11/6/17.
2. www.webmd/mentalhealth/addiction/features/12-health-risks-of-heavy-drinking. Accessed online 11/6/17.
3. http://www.cancer.org.au/preventing-cancer/reduce-your-risk/quit-smoking.html. Accessed online 11/6/17.
4. www.drugfreeworld.org/drugfacts. Accessed online 11/6/17.

5. https://thiswayup.org.au/. Accessed online 22/2/18.
6. APS (2015) Survey of Australians' social media usage. https://www.headsup.org.au/docs/default-source/default-document-library/stress-and-wellbeing-in-australia-report.pdf?sfvrsn=7f08274d_4. Accessed online 1/8/18.
7. https://allpsych.com/tests/diagnostic/sexualaddiction/. Accessed online 13/6/17.

CHAPTER 12

1. Hay, Louise L.(1984) *You Can Heal Your Life.* Specialist Publications: Australia.
2. Seligman, M. (2011) *Flourish.* Random House: Australia.
3. McKay, M. & Fanning, P. (1991) *Prisoners of Belief.* New Harbinger: USA.
4. www.dianahutchison.com/shop Core Beliefs inventory.

CHAPTER 13

1. Cornelius, H. & Faire, S. (2006) 2nd Ed. *Everyone Can Win:*

Responding to Conflict Constructively. Simon & Schuster (Australia) Pty Ltd: Sydney.
2. Kidman, A. (1990) *Managing Love and Hate: A Self Help Manual.* Biochemical and General Services: St Leonards, Australia.

CHAPTER 14

1. Hutchison, D.E. (2018) *Setting Yourself Free.* 2nd ed. DoctorZed Publishing: Australia.
2. Cloud, H. & Townsend, John (2004) *Boundaries: To Take Control of Your Life.* Cengage Learning Inc: USA.
3. www.dianahutchison.com/shop You can download Chapter 7 on goal setting for free.
4. Miller, Caroline A. (2017) *Getting Grit: The evidence-based approach to cultivating passion, perseverance and purpose.* Sounds True: USA.
5. www.dianahutchison.com/shop You can download a blank decisional balance here.

6. Seligman, M.E.P. (1990) *Learned Optimism.* Random House: Australia.
7. Seigel, Daniel (2010) *Mindsight: The New Science Of Personal Transformation.* Bantam Books: USA.
8. Seligman, M.E.P. (2011) *Flourish.* Random House: Australia.

Other Titles

Setting Yourself Free DoctorZed Publishing
(2nd edition)
Genre: Self-help
Available in print and ebook.
Welcome to the human experience—and your guide to a better life.
Setting Yourself Free is your practical guide to self-change. With some encouragement and the right tools, you can take the first steps to a new life.
"A highly practical and to-the-point book that will help kick-start and maintain an effective personal change program."

Anthony M. Grant, PhD, Director, Coaching Psychology Unit, University of Sydney

Back Cover Material

As a young adult, you aim to get the most out of life. You want to have awesome relationships, an awesome career, and awesome experiences. When you're working to achieve these goals, the best place to start is with yourself.

Whatever your worries, and wherever you're starting from, this clear and friendly guidebook gives you all the tools you need to be awesome. From laying a solid foundation, to building your goals, to reaching new heights, you can become who you always wanted to be.

Counsellor and life coach Diana Hutchison addresses all your questions about setting healthy boundaries, saving for a home, even ensuring a balanced diet.

By following her simple steps, you will quickly learn how to create an awesome you!

Diana Hutchison has a background in psychology and is now a counsellor and life coach in Adelaide, South Australia. She specialises in grief and loss, relationship counselling and health and well-being. She is also an NLP Master Practitioner.

Learn more at www.dianahutchison.com

www.ingramcontent.com/pod-product-compliance
Lightning Source LLC
Chambersburg PA
CBHW011737220426
43661CB00062B/2874